Walking
THE PATHWAY
OF PRAYER

Walking
THE PATHWAY
OF PRAYER

VIOLET O. COX

Xulon Press
2301 Lucien Way #415
Maitland, FL 32751
407.339.4217
www.xulonpress.com

Unless otherwise indicated, scripture quotations are taken from The King James Version (KJV) – *public domain*. Used by permission. All right reserved.

Printed in the United States of America

ISBN 9781545611722

DEDICATION

This book is dedicated to my adult daughter Lee-Amor who inspired me to pray and to write about prayer. Never will I forget her words, she was almost three years of age, "Mommy God will make you happy!"

I also want to recognize the many individuals who have influenced my prayer journey in so many different ways: Dr. Myron Edmonds, Pastor Cameron Bowen, all of my prayer partners on the prayer lines, and my "travel prayer friends," Doris Hall, Malinda Woods, Barbara Davis and Clara Parrish – remembering the tedious hours we drove from one city to the next bathed in prayer!

Finally, it is truly to the precious memory of my late husband Dr. Leon Cox, whose life was a testament of prayer, that I dedicate this volume.

V. O. Cox

TABLE OF CONTENTS

INTRODUCTION

"God speaks to us through His Word: we respond to Him through our prayers, and he always listens to us."
E.G White.

I grew up in a Christian home. My parents prayed in the morning in the evening and before every meal was eaten. They prayed with their children and over them while they slept. As a child, I thought praying was a parental behavior. I remember kneeling by my bedside while I repeated my first prayer modeled after every word uttered by my mother. But it was not until around the age of nine or ten that I "tried out" my own prayer. One day I saw a pair of pretty green shoes displayed in a shoe store. I thought to myself, "I'll see if God

"Ah Lord God! Behold, You have made the heavens and the earth by Your great power and by Your outstretched arm! Nothing is too difficult for You. . . ."

Jeremiah 32: 17 (NASB)

God Hears Every Prayer

would let me have those shoes!" I don't remember my exact words, but the prayer may have been something like this. "Dear God if you really hear little children's prayers, then let me have that pair of green shoes, you know, the ones in the shoe store with the white leaf on each side." I don't think I had to have them. I'm not even sure why I picked the green shoes. Green was not even my favorite color! I simply wanted to find out whether God would pay attention to me. So I prayed in my heart for the shoes. Almost a day or so later, my mother came home from the shoe store with the exact pair of green shoes. My heart raced with with delight, as I

God Hears You

"It was about planting the seed of faith in my heart. The faith that gives the assurance "Yes, God hears you!"

shouted, "He answers! He answers!" That was my first independent contact with God through prayer. I believe God knew I did not need the shoes. But He knew that I needed desperately to have the confirmation in my heart that He would hear and answer my prayer. It was not about the shoes. It was about planting the seed of faith in my heart. The faith that gives the assurance "Yes, God hears you!" So it was from this first childhood encounter with God that my pathway of prayer began. Unfortunately, I cannot say I was always diligent in prayer, but nevertheless, the journey had begun.

"We must live our prayers if they are to be answered."

E.G White

God Hears You

Now many decades later, I embrace the truth that prayer is as essential to the Christian's spiritual life, as air is to the physical body. You cannot exist a moment without it! Prayer is much more than asking God for a pair of green shoes! It is a conscious awareness of being in His presence every waking moment of life! There were times in my adult life that I struggled to reach the full spiritual settling that God is fundamentally available and interested in every aspect of life. This fact became a reality for me very early one morning as I stood at a window gazing up at the skies just before full day break. To me it is the most incredibly peaceful

"The Presence of God"

"I experienced an amazing settling of peace in my heart. . . .The peace I felt was extraordinary. . . .God had spoken to me. I had experienced prayer!"

part of the day. My husband had recently passed away. I was still a new-comer to the city I now call home. At the time, I hardly knew my neighbors by their first or even last names, and I had not yet formed relationships in my new church. I was alone, or so it seemed to me. In my reverie of thoughts, my eyes were drawn towards the wide expanse of the heavens that seemed to speak to my soul. Somehow I felt drawn into the presence of God. I opened my mouth and started crying out to Him for some kind of assurance. In my desperate cry, I experienced an amazing settling of peace in my heart. I felt as if He had spoken to me personally!

"Dig deep and lean in to the truth – the truth of who you are and what [God] has created you to offer to the world."

Priscilla Shirer

"The Presence of God"

The peace I felt was extraordinary. Immediately I knew that I was not alone. God had spoken to me. I had experienced prayer!

We can consciously experience the awareness of communing with God in several modes. We can do so silently allowing our hearts to link with His or we can experience His presence through praise as we stand in awe of His Majestic glory. I have had many direct encounters with God as a result of prayer.

There were times (many of these) when I prayed but failed to wait for His response. Those were the times when he allowed me to suffer the consequences of answering my own

Prayer is a Journey

"It's an amazing journey. . . .I never cease to be astounded by the fact that God is always willing and ready to respond to every little prayer of mine whatever the situation!"

prayers! Valuable lessons! Because of these many personal encounters with God that I have experienced through prayer, I feel impelled to share my prayer journey in this book. It's an amazing journey that I take on a daily basis. I never cease to be astounded by the fact that God is always willing and ready to respond to every little prayer of mine whatever the situation! I hope that everyone who reads this little volume may be encouraged to begin or to continue to enrich their own journey of prayer.

Writing about prayer has opened the door that leads me further and further along the path to a deeper and wider experience of talking with God.

"Integrity means being the same underneath as we are on the outside."

Priscilla Shirer

Prayer is a Journey

"Whether interceding, praising Him, or sitting silently in His presence offering spontaneous thanks, we can be assured that He hears every prayer."

One of the experiences that I am beginning to enjoy is recognizing the voice of God! This has been one of my breakthrough moments in walking the pathway of prayer. I have to confess that many times I've mistaken His voice and ended up taking a faulty exist along the pathway. In moments like those, He calls out to me again and I hear Him. This is what makes this journey of prayer so very exciting!

In the first section of this book, I share with the reader a series of short chapters that describe different types of prayers and the effects of prayer on our lives. Whether interceding, praising Him, or just sitting silently

> *"Angels mark our prayers and influence us for good."*
>
> *E .G. White*

Prayer is a Journey

in His presence offering spontaneous thanks, we can be assured that He hears every prayer.

The second section of the book presents some of my personal real life answers to prayers. This section highlights the reality of how God truly responds to situations in our daily lives. Some of these personal encounters may be hair raising at times, but they all speak to the ever abiding presence of God in our day to day experiences. So to the individual who is wrestling with the question of whether God really answers prayers, this section will remove all doubts in a very real and personal way.

1

TEACH ME
TO PRAY

For years I performed the perfunctory prayer. It was my habitual morning and evening act. My daily ritual! The words were the same. The length of my prayers was the same. I was adept at these rituals. It was not difficult to multitask between my utterances. While "praying," my mind wandered off to plan mundane events or to ruminate on past activities. How was that possible? Obviously, my prayer experience was shallow. I had to admit that my

Teach Me to Pray

"I knew the appropriate theological terminology, but internally, I also knew that my prayers were short in effect, focus and sincerity."

relationship with God was not passionate even though I led a "prayer-filled" life! I had to face reality. I did not know how to pray. Yes, I knew the right words to say. I knew the correct sequence of thought especially if I had to "perform" the public prayer. I knew the appropriate theological terminology, but internally, I also knew that my prayers were short in effect, focus and sincerity. Did God ever hear and answer any of my prayers? Yes He did! Fortunately, He does not always deal with us in the way that we deserve!

But this is not my unique experience. This se*nse of "lack of positive effect" pr*ayer was most likely experienced by Jesus' disciples.

"Every promise in the word of God furnishes us with subject matter for prayer."

E. G. White

Teach Me to Pray

"When the disciples asked Jesus in childlike earnestness "Lord teach us to pray," their request was born out of a deep recognition of their own weak and paltry expressions of prayer. . . .they had not yet acquired the "skill" of praying."

When the disciples asked Jesus in childlike earnestness "Lord teach us to pray," their request was born out of a deep recognition of their own weak and paltry expressions of prayer. Even though they were in the very presence of the One through whom prayers are made possible, they had not yet acquired the "skill" of praying. They observed the passion and sincerity of Christ's interactions with His Heavenly Father. They saw the glow of satisfaction on His face and His renewed strength after these prayer encounters. But by contrast, they also saw how ineffective their own prayers had been. They recognized their immediate need to learn how to

26

Hear my prayer O Lord, and give ear to my cry; hold not your peace at my tears.

Psalm 39:12

Teach Me to Pray

pray, hence their apparently simplistic but most profound request, *"Lord, teach us to pray. . . ."* (Luke 11:1).

Our situation today is no different from that of the disciples. Most of us have been church-goers for many years if not all of our lives, and still lack the enthusiasm for praying. Why is this so? Perhaps we don't truly understand the power and significance of prayer. I have heard some individuals say that praying is "old school." It is not necessary to pray because God already knows your heart and He knows what you need so the whole act of praying is redundant. Wow! They simply don't get it! They have not grasped what prayer is all

Teach Me to Pray

"Prayer is the opening of the heart to God as to a friend. . . .Prayer does not bring God down to us, but brings us up to Him."

E.G. White

about. So what is it? First, it's not a complicated task. It is rather a refreshing experience. Look at how Ellen White puts it:

"Prayer is the opening of the heart to God as to a friend. Not that it is necessary, in order to make known to God what we are, but in order to enable us to receive Him. Prayer does not bring God down to us, but brings us up to Him."[1]

In my recent prayer journey, I uncovered three key elements about prayer: It is a direct link to heaven; it is a divine invitation and it is a special system. In attempting to understand

"If there were more praying among us, more exercise of a living faith, and less dependence upon someone else to have an experience for us, we would be far in advance of where we are today in spiritual intelligence."

E. G. White

Teach Me to Pray

"It is the single most powerful weapon the weakest Christian possesses. It is the counteractive force against fear."

these three keys I had to revamp many of my preconceived notions about God. I have to admit that even in my adult years I still held on to my childhood concept of God as someone far away and with whom I communicated at set times. It was only within recent years that I jettisoned that faulty concept and realized that He is my constant companion. As I began the process of learning to interact with God, I realized that He too desires to interact with me. Once I understood this it became easy for me to tap into that direct link to heaven through prayer.

Call to me and I will answer you and tell you great and unsearchable things you do not know.

Jeremiah 33:3(NIV)

Teach Me to Pray

"Prayer. . . is the vertical grounding we establish with God so that we can be horizontally connected with each other."

Prayer is a direct link to Heaven

Prayer is an integrated communication system between us and God; it is our direct line to heaven. It is the process that allows us to talk to God unhindered. It is the single most powerful weapon the weakest Christian possesses. It is the counteractive force against fear. It is central to the Christian's existence. It is the master key to the heart of God. It is that vertical grounding we establish with God so that we can be horizontally connected with each other. It is a symbol of how the cross of Calvary connects heaven with earth! It is what links us to God!

"If my people who are called by my name, will humble themselves and pray and seek my face and turn from their wicked ways, then will I hear from heaven, and I will forgive their sin and will heal their land.

2 Chronicles 7:14 (NIV)

Teach Me to Pray

In the act of prayer, God converses with us through His Word and we in turn offer our responses through prayer. Therefore, prayer means talking and listening to God! This integrated communication process allows us to speak directly with Him as we would in a person-to-person phone call. Today we have smart phones – and all sorts of communication devices to help us stay in perpetual contact with each other. The social media allows us to blog, tweet, twitter and text each other in real time. Thank God for these very necessary items of technology! Sometimes these devices serve as the only means of communicating and in some cases the last link between love ones. During the 9/11 Terrorists' Attack on the United States of America, one young man who lost his wife along with all on board Flight 93 over Philadelphia, was able to maintain contact with her on the doomed flight right up to the final moments, via her cellular phone. She was not only able to convey to him perhaps the only accurate account of the nefarious activities on board that ill-fated flight, but also her last words of love. These words no doubt are eternally etched on his heart. How thankful we are for cell phones! We may even wonder how we ever managed to survive without them! But as sophisticated as the technology

Teach Me to Pray

"God's channel of communication is never blocked from His end; it may be from ours!"

is, it frequently fails! We experience static on the line! Sometimes the call is dropped and we are left wondering what the caller said. Sometimes the service is interrupted! How often have you called to speak to someone and you are greeted instead with a recording "your party is unavailable please leave a message and your call will be answered as soon as possible," and you hang up in disappointment! But here is some good news! God's channel of communication is never blocked from His end; it may be from ours! When you access His system you never experience static on the line even though there are storms in your life. You never experience a

Then you will call on me and come and pray to me, and I will listen to you.

Jeremiah 29:12 (NIV)

dropped call because His line of contact is never crossed or overloaded. When you are burdened, running low on your fund of faith, and you are wondering how to reach Him, His service continues to be available to you. He does not disconnect His prayer line because you missed contact with Him. He is the one and only accessible God! When you find yourself in a broken place filled with despair and doubt, His communication system remains intact. He is always available! A mother gave her teenage daughter a smart-phone so that the two could stay in touch – their safety mechanism! However, the plan as good as it was, fell short the day

"Prayer is a divinely appointed invitation. The only response required is to reach out through faith and talk to God."

the young girl forgot the phone on the school bus. How frantic the mother became when she was unable to reach her daughter at the set time for their contact! We have no need to fear about losing contact with God. As the common cliché states, "He's only a prayer away." However as in the case of this young girl, the flaw comes when we forget to maintain contact with God. But in spite of our forgetfulness, he still invites us to call out to Him!

Prayer is a divine invitation

Prayer is a divinely appointed invitation. The only response required

> *"Faith in a prayer-hearing God will make a prayer-loving Christian."*
>
> *Andrew Murray*

Teach Me to Pray

is to reach out through faith and talk to God. He invites us to talk to Him as often as we dare. As a matter of fact, it was God who made the first move towards us. Isaiah 43:1 says "*. . .Fear not, for I have redeemed you; I have summoned you by name; you are mine.*"(NIV). This is what makes God the kind and loving Father He is. He is constantly reminding us that it does not matter what we have done, or where we've been, we are still His!

When Prince William and Kate Middleton of Great Britain were planning their wedding, many known dignitaries across the world received invitations, and just as many did not. Still millions of lesser known persons

Teach Me to Pray

including you and I did not enter the periphery of their thoughts when these invitations were being composed and we were not offended, in fact we never expected to be invited! But to think that the Great King of the universe, the Creator, the Savior of the entire world has personally issued a special invitation to each of us with our names carefully embossed simply boggles the mind! The invitation is for us to come into His throne room at any time, with any situation, simply come just as we are! Note His very poignant invitation vividly recorded *"Come, all you who are thirsty, come to the waters; and you who have no money, come, buy and eat! Come,*

Teach Me to Pray

buy wine and milk without money and without cost. Why spend money on what is not bread, and your labor on what does not satisfy? Listen, listen to me, and eat what is good, and your soul will delight in the richest of fare. Give ear and come to me; hear me that your soul may live. . ." (Isaiah 55:1-3 NIV emphasis added).

Have you ever invited someone to dinner only to suffer disappointment because they were unable come for whatever reason? Even though profuse apologies might have been extended to you, somewhere in your heart you still experienced a sense of hurt or perhaps embarrassment. You may even have made a mental note not

Teach Me to Pray

". . .He does not give up on us even when we repeatedly turn Him down! The beauty in all of this is that God always makes that first move towards us."

to extend an invitation to that person again. Imagine how it must pain the heart of God when we turn our backs on the gracious invitation He offers to us! But He does not give up on us even when we repeatedly turn Him down! The beauty in all of this is that God always makes that first move towards us. Jeremiah the prophet was incarcerated when he received one of the warmest invitations recorded *"Call to me, and I will answer you and tell you great and unsearchable things you do not know."*(Jeremiah 33:3 NIV). Furthermore, Jesus reiterated the invitation again in Matthew 7:7 *"Ask and it will be given to you; seek and you will find; knock and the*

"We must begin to believe that God, in the mystery of prayer, has entrusted us with a force that can move the Heavenly world and can bring its power down to earth."

Andrew Murray

Teach Me to Pray

"God has graciously invited you and me into his presence and has extended to us the promise fulfilment of every need!"

door will be opened to you." This is one of the most generous invitations ever given. Imagine this. God has graciously invited you and me into his presence and has extended to us the promise fulfilment of every need! No disappointment here! There is no system on earth that offers such a guarantee.

Prayer is a special system

Prayer is a special system established by God. It guarantees our ability to stay in His presence. Before sin, our first parents, Adam and Eve, maintained an intimate face-to-face interaction with Him. When sin came

47

"Prayer does not fit us for the greater work; prayer is the greater work."

Oswald Chambers

in and marred this direct system, God withdrew His visible presence. But He did not take away the line of contact. He established a sacrificial system of prayer. When He sent His Son Jesus Christ as the life-line between earth and heaven, so graciously demonstrated on the cross, all atonement symbols of His sacrifice ceased. It was no longer necessary to pray to the Father through priests, or to offer special oblations in the form of animals. The system of personal and private prayer was established through Jesus Christ. Yes, He is the One who is truly fit to teach us how to pray, and through whom, we have this splendid invitation to come boldly to

Teach Me to Pray

"... He will hear and respond to every prayer uttered by His children."

the throne of Grace. Thank God for the wonderful and glorious accommodation of prayer!

In summary, God says emphatically that He will hear and respond to every prayer uttered by His children - *"The eyes of the Lord are upon the righteous, and his ears are open unto their cry"* (Psalm 34:15).

1 E. G White Steps to Christ p. 93

"I have been driven many times upon my knees by the overwhelming conviction that I had nowhere else to go."

Abraham Lincoln

2

THE INSTANTANEOUS PRAYER

I t was a bleak rainy afternoon. I was nearing the hair-pin bend notoriously known as "Dead Man's Curve," a treacherous section of I-90 in Cleveland Ohio. This curve is every motorist's night-mare. The eighteen-wheeler roared past my Oldsmobile seemingly from out of no-where. Its illegal speed created such a suctioning pressure between my car and its giant wheels, that for one sickening split second I experienced the guzzling effect of being

The Instantaneous Prayer

"The prayer uttered under those circumstances when there is no time to form fancy sequential utterances or to bargain with God; the prayer blurted out in those moments when you are staring death in the face is the ejaculatory expression of the soul."

sucked into the massive under-belly of this iron monster. I heard a voice, I later recognized as my own, "JESUS!" Immediately, my car settled back on the road. I was saved! What a prayer! What an answer! The prayer uttered under those circumstances when there is no time to form fancy sequential utterances or to bargain with God; the prayer blurted out in those moments when you are staring death in the face is the ejaculatory expression of the soul. In linguistics an ejaculatory response is defined as any emotional utterance that falls outside the normal linguistic structure of the language. It can consist of a single word or a short phrase. This kind of prayer is not the

"Daniel was a man of prayer who considered it so important that he would not stop praying even to save his own life."

Ron Halvorsen

The Instantaneous Prayer

hasty ritualistic prayer one sometimes renders when pressed for time, or when performed as a salve for a guilty conscience. In fact, that kind of prayer or might I say ritual is an insult to God!

Every morning for the last nine or ten years, a group of us would gather for prayer sessions by teleconference. I am always blessed by the prayers of these spirit-filled individuals. Frequently one would hear unrehearsed expressions of "Glory to God!" or "Hallelujah!" uttered by some individuals as they felt compelled by the Holy Spirit. During one of these prayer sessions I heard the quiet passionate voice of one troubled

The Instantaneous Prayer

"I will answer them before they even call to me. While they are still talking about their needs, I will go ahead and answer their prayers."
Isaiah 65:24 NLT

individual quietly urging, "Mercy!" The short outburst of this poor soul spoke volumes about her circumstances. The Bible has recorded many of these focused yet unrehearsed prayers that evoked on-the-spot action from God. The immediacy of His response to the soul's aspiration is most clearly recorded *"I will answer them before they even call to me. While they are still talking about their needs, I will go ahead and answer their prayers."* (Isaiah 65:24 NLT).

Peter had this "instant-prayer-instant-response" experience. He had taken bold steps that eventful night recorded in Mathew 14, to dare to "walk on the water" at the invitation

"Even in His extreme weakness, Christ's knowledge of and dedication to God's Word was so strong that His spiritual reflexes took over."

Ron Halvorsen

The Instantaneous Prayer

". . .immediately Jesus reached out and bore him to safety. What an effective prayer! Parenthetically, I like to imagine that the hand of Jesus was already stretched out waiting for him [Peter] to grasp it! That's what God meant when He said 'And it shall come to pass, that before they call, I will answer; and while they are yet speaking, I will hear.'"

(Isaiah 65:24).

of Jesus. The billowing waves roared all around him. His once certain steps on the transparent but firm watery walk-way now became tentative as he froze with fear of the roaring winds and billowing sea that surrounded him. His frail humanity was no match for the elements. All of his experiences as a fisherman of the deep seas spoke to him of his imminent death. Instantaneously he exclaimed *"Lord save me"* (Matthew 14: 30) and immediately Jesus reached out and bore him to safety. What an effective prayer! Parenthetically, I like to imagine that the hand of Jesus was already stretched out waiting for him to grasp it! That's what God meant

"I know of no better thermometer to your spiritual temperature than this, the measure of the intensity of your prayer."

Charles H. Spurgeon

The Instantaneous Prayer

when He said *"And it shall come to pass, that before they call, I will answer; and while they are yet speaking, I will hear."* (Isaiah 65:24). Some people no doubt would focus on Peter's lack of faith that brought him to that near death experience, but look at his rebounding trust in Jesus' power to save! This was the kind of faith that had emboldened him earlier to step out of his boat and walk on to the water. Even though faltering momentarily as he succumbed to fear, you have to admit that it was the same faith that caused him to call out instantly to Jesus in his moment of extreme fear.

The Instantaneous Prayer

"The heart wrenching prayer that erupts from a person in deep distress is the one that penetrates the heart of God immediately!"

But let me add here that the instantaneous prayer is not entirely unrehearsed. I believe that this kind of prayer takes on its unique effect based on two important events: (1) the prior experiential encounters the individual has had with God and (2) the immediate sincerity of the soul. It seems to me that it is impossible for one to utter a prayer to God without some prior connection with Him whether directly or indirectly. It was the famous preacher Spurgeon who said that the best form of prayer is that which is uttered in a cry. No wonder God invites us to *"Call unto me, and I will answer. . . ."* (Jer. 33:3). The heart wrenching prayer that erupts from a

> *"A true prayer is an inventory of needs, a catalog of necessities, an exposure of secret wounds, a revelation of hidden poverty."*
>
> *Charles H. Spurgeon*

The Instantaneous Prayer

person in deep distress is the one that penetrates the heart of God immediately! It was nine o'clock in the evening. A group of us met on the prayer line for evening devotions, the facilitator asked if there were any prayer requests. There was silence, and then an unfamiliar voice cried out "God save my child." Immediately one individual commenced to pray over the situation; before the season of prayer had expired, the unfamiliar voice responded. "My child is okay now."

The cry emitted from the heart of this mother was actually her urgent prayer to God, a prayer that was echoed and confirmed by another

The Instantaneous Prayer

praying soul. We later learned from the mother that her daughter was diagnosed with a dreadful muscular disorder that frequently caused severe pain sometimes requiring hospitalization. That night when she dialed the prayer line, the pain was the worst her child had ever experienced. The moment the short prayer request was uttered by the mother, the daughter received immediate relief from the pain. What a mighty God!

David expresses confidence in the fact that God hears the deep cries of the soul when he says *"I cried out to God for help; I cried out to God to hear me."* (Psalm 77:1 NIV emphasis added). Perhaps one of the

The Instantaneous Prayer

"The malefactor on the cross instantly recognized three profound truths: (1) the Savior of the world was on the cross next to him, (2) death for him was certain and (3) he needed to be saved right at that moment."

most poignant cries ever uttered was that of the thief hanging on the cross next to Jesus. This man's brief conversation with Jesus on the cross is not duly listed among the most common prayers in the Bible. For one thing, his situation was despicable. He was about to die, no doubt a just death, for his crimes. However, this malefactor on the cross instantly recognized three profound truths: (1) the Savior of the world was on the cross next to him, (2) death for him was certain and (3) he needed to be saved right at that moment. These truths flooded his soul like a flash of lightning causing every fiber of his being to burst into the heart wrenching plea of *"Jesus,*

The Instantaneous Prayer

remember me. . ." (Luke 23:42 NIV). Why didn't this man ask specifically to be forgiven of the crime or crimes that caused him to be on the cross? Was he presumptuous in thinking that Jesus would save him? Actually, bound up in his hasty prayer was his recognition of Christ's redeeming power to pardon from sin. This was the faith Jesus recognized in the man's prayer. Christ on the cross was the visible manifestation of global forgiveness for the entire human race. Right then, the man instantly seized the opportunity. He did not have the time to utter long speeches. His longing soul spoke volumes that his lips could not utter. Within his urgent

The Instantaneous Prayer

"Circumstances that require immediate action, of necessity, call for emergency flares from the soul that supersede any vocalizations the lips may utter."

aspiration was encapsulated the request "Lord, Jesus, forgive me of my past and bring me into a glorious future with you forever!"

Circumstances that require immediate action, of necessity, call for emergency flares from the soul that supersede any vocalizations the lips may utter. Recall the scene with Nehemiah in the presence of the king. It was a time of deep distress for Nehemiah; he was overcome with grief because of the condition of his home city Judah (Nehemiah 2). Standing before the king in the execution of his duties, Nehemiah could not conceal the sadness of his heart. The insightful king immediately sensed

"Answer me when I call to you, my righteous God. Give me relief from my distress; have mercy upon me and hear my prayer."

Psalm 4:1 NIV

The Instantaneous Prayer

that something was wrong, hence his rather searching question: "Why does your face look so sad when you are not ill? This can be nothing but sadness of heart."(Nehemiah 2:2 NIH). Nehemiah quickly explained to the king the reason for his sadness to which the king's ready response was ". . .What is it you want (?). . ." (Nehemiah 2: 4).

He did not trust his lips to utter his own thoughts to God. It was one of those moments when "deep cried out to deep." Nehemiah in his own words recorded *"Then I prayed to the God of heaven, and I answered the king."* In one breath he talked to God and immediately after to the king.

The Instantaneous Prayer

". . .Nehemiah's soul erupted before God in advance of his lips executing a response to the king's inquiry."

Now that had to be the briefest of prayers! For one thing, he could not keep the king waiting. To do so would have been construed as rudeness. Secondly, he did not have time to embark on any long sequential prayer. But before he dared to respond to the king right away, he had to reach out to the King of Kings from the depths of his innermost being. He could not afford to answer the king, Artaxerxes, from any selfish motivation because the fate of a nation was at stake here! So Nehemiah's soul erupted before God in advance of his lips executing a response to the king's inquiry. No doubt, the brief prayer he directed towards heaven, moved the heart of

> *"When my life was ebbing away, I remembered you, Lord, and my prayer rose to you, to your holy temple."*
>
> *Jonah 2:7 NIV*

"God listens to the soul. The mouth merely speaks what the soul has already uttered to God!"

the earthly king Artaxerxes in such a manner that he, Nehemiah, was granted carte blanche to travel and to start the process of rebuilding his nation! E.G. White states:

". . .to pray as Nehemiah prayed in his hour of need is a resource at the command of the Christian under circumstances when other forms of prayer may be impossible."[1]

God listens to the soul. The mouth merely speaks what the soul has already uttered to God! Spontaneous prayers are those kinds of prayers that we activate at any time or any situation. Sometimes these are

The Instantaneous Prayer

prayers of help for someone in need, a spontaneous outburst of praise and thanksgiving or prayers coming from a heart gripped by contrition. Whatever the circumstance, wherever you are, this type of prayer calls to your attention the fact that our God is everywhere, all knowing, all sufficient and easily accessible. This type of prayer renders helpless the excuse that one could not pray because it was an inappropriate time to pray. Look at Nehemiah's position one more time. He was in the presence of the king. His job, his very life could have been at stake. But between the king's question and his response, there was enough time for him to talk to God!

The Instantaneous Prayer

Another dramatic declaration of the instantaneous prayer is captured in the story of Samson's last hours. The backdrop to this story depicts a scene of noise and commotion typical of bacchanals. Hardly a scene for prayer. We get a visual of the blinded Samson at the finale of his life standing silently in stark contrast to his location. He was a spectacle of mockery. Everyone had turned out to get a good laugh at the now disgraced and blinded ex- hero! *"Now the temple was crowded with men and women; all the rulers of the Philistines were there, and on the roof were about three thousand men and women watching Samson perform."*

The Instantaneous
Prayer

*"With great strength
and resolute spirit,
Samson emits his
strongest aspiration
to God".*

(Judges 16:27 emphasis added). Can you see this? All kinds of people were present. Those who could not fit in the wide expanse of the dance hall, literally dangled from the roof just to get a glimpse of Samson performing in a most ignominious fashion. In between his performances - and he was about to give the greatest one of his life, "... *Samson prayed to the Lord, 'Sovereign Lord, remember me. Please, God, strengthen me just once more. ...'* " (Judges 16: 28 NIV emphasis added). With great strength and resolute spirit, Samson emits his strongest aspiration to God. Caught up in the strength of this type of prayer Samson was emboldened to the point

The Instantaneous Prayer

where he was able to contend with and destroy more of his enemies than he had done in his life time. That is the type of power that permeates the instantaneous prayer!

1 E. G. White Prophets and Kings p. 631

"Prayer delights God's ear: it melts His Heart; and opens His hand. God cannot deny a praying soul."

Thomas Watson

3

THE SECRET PRAYER

"Private communion with God is the time when you get real with Him."

The biggest victories over personal besetting sins are won in the secret prayer closet. Private communion with God is the time when you get real with Him. This is that place where you take off your mask – your public face – and you tell Him the things you would not dare to disclose to another. You freely admit "Lord, I'm a liar. I'm a thief! I'm a slanderer!" Now let's be frank. Are these the types of disclosures you would readily share with another person and

"Prayer is not learned in a classroom but in the closet.

E. M. Bounds

The Secret Prayer

still maintain "face?" Certainly not! But after disclosing to God you can be sure that He will not scorn you, or talk about you behind your back. More than that, He alone provides you with the solution and the victory over your sins!

Secret prayer is very important; in solitude the soul is laid bare to the inspecting eye of God, and every motive is scrutinized. Secret prayer! How precious! The soul communing with God! Secret prayer is to be heard only by the prayer-hearing God. No curious ear is to receive the burden of such petition.[1]

The Secret Prayer

"It's within the confines of this space that you can be totally transparent in His presence. It's where the weakest soul can find incredible strength to stand up against the landmines of the enemy."

I have found three essential elements in secret communion with God. In the secret prayer closet with God, there is strength, there is solace, and there is anointing.

Strength in the Secret Space

Secret communion with God brings the assurance of renewed strength in every sense of the word. It's within the confines of this space that you can be totally transparent in His presence. It's the place where weakest soul can find incredible strength to stand up against the landmines of the enemy. As a human being, Jesus spent many hours in secret prayer so that

81

"The first purpose of prayer is to bring you and God together."

Ron Halvorsen

The Secret Prayer

He could receive wisdom and power. Why should it be any different for us? After all He is our example!

"When new and great trials were before Him, He would steal away to the solitude of the mountains and pass the entire night in prayer to His Heavenly Father."[2]

Christ taught us by example how to gain power over difficult situations. The Bible gives a clear description of His secret prayer encounters. *"And in the morning, rising up a great while before day, he went out, and departed into a solitary place, and there prayed."* (Mark 1:35) The

The Secret Prayer

previous day, Jesus had been healing and blessing all sorts of people. It started off with healing Simon's mother-in-law. Later on in the day the entire city brought their sick and afflicted to Him for healing. Most likely, fatigue from the day's activities had set in. He needed time alone to regroup. He needed to be away from the crowd, even away from His loyal friends – the disciples. He needed time out from His closest friends. He needed that special one-on-one with His Father. So He got up very early in the morning, "a great while before day" possibly around three o'clock and retreated to a "solitary place." What is this solitary place? First, a

The Secret Prayer

solitary place is lonely. It's a place away from the beaten path. It's a place void of human contact. Why would such a place be a prime location to pray? E. G. White suggests that because Christ was a

"He [Jesus] was wholly dependent upon God, and in the secret place of prayer He sought divine strength, that He might go forth braced for duty and trial. . ."

". . . sharer in our needs and weaknesses, He was wholly dependent upon God, and in the secret place of prayer He sought divine strength, that He might go forth braced for duty and trial. . . .In communion with God He could unburden the sorrows that were crushing Him. Here He found comfort and joy."[3]

85

O, let the place of secret prayer become to me the most beloved spot on earth.

Andrew Murray

The Secret Prayer

This tells me that Jesus also needed a "special space" where He could be transparent with His father. I imagine that this is where he unlocked every chamber of His heart to the Father. Now the Bible does not specifically share the details of the contents of His private prayers to the Father, except in Gethsemane, but we do know that these times of intimacy with the Father provided Him with the boost of strength He needed for the day! He needed this mental space where He could unleash all the contents of His heart to His Heavenly Father!

The Secret Prayer

"... A place where we are so broken that the only possible way out is to call on Him. That is our solitary place! That is the place Christ frequently visited on our behalf. He was the proof positive that God dwells in the solitary places of our experiences and we do not need to be afraid to seek Him there."

A Solitary Place

A solitary place is descriptive of our human condition and our acute need! In His unprecedented efforts to save us, God sometimes allows us to be in a place of loneliness. A place of desertion. A place where we are so broken that the only possible way out is to call on Him. That is our solitary place! That is the place Christ frequently visited on our behalf. He was the proof positive that God dwells in the solitary places of our experiences and we do not need to be afraid to seek Him there. That's why the Psalmist declares *"He that dwelleth in the secret place of the most High shall*

The Secret Prayer

abide under the shadow of the Almighty." (Ps.91:1 emphasis added). This tells us that the solitary place is not a place of abandonment or confinement. Rather, it's a place where action begins! You see, once Jesus had completed His purpose in that solitary place – communing with His Father – then His disciples "found Him." Now renewed in strength, fully energized and equipped, He was ready for action! He outlined His plans for the new day, *"Let us go into the next towns that I may preach there also: for therefore came I forth."* (Mark 1:38 emphasis added). From that secret place with God, you always emerge with a well-crafted plan of action!

The Secret Prayer

There are times in our grief when we long for a type of consolation that transcends any words of comfort that another human being can provide. This deep consoling can only be found within the innermost pockets of deep communion with the Almighty. Anne Frank, a German Jewish refugee diarist noted in her diary entry of February 23, 1944, that the best remedy for those who are afraid, lonely or unhappy is to be alone with nature and God. The Psalmist David experienced this solitude with God repeatedly; no wonder he was able to declare in perfect meter, *"The heavens declare the glory of God; and the firmament sheweth his*

The Secret Prayer

"God alone is the comforter of the soul that is hurting, but we have to intentionally set up a meeting with Him. We must purposely get away from the mundane tasks of life and seek solace with our Heavenly father."

handywork." (Psalms 19:1). Maria Saunders in her book "Come with me to the Secret Place: The Place to find Solace" acknowledges that alcohol, sex, gambling even money do not bring solace to the aching soul. God alone is the comforter of the soul that is hurting, but we have to intentionally set up a meeting with Him. We must purposely get away from the mundane tasks of life and seek solace with our Heavenly father. Whatever time of day or night we choose does not matter. We simply need to follow the pattern outlined by Jesus Christ, *"But when you pray, go to your room close the door and pray to your Father who is unseen. Then your father, who*

"When the devil sees a man or woman who really believes in prayer, who knows how to pray, and who really does pray, and, above all, when he sees a whole church on its face before God in prayer, he trembles as much as he ever did, for he knows that his day in that church or community is at an end."

R. A. Torrey

The Secret Prayer

"Close the door" moves you to a place of additional privacy. Closing the door is how you sound-proof your mind from the externals of life."

sees what is done in secret, will reward you." (Matthew 6:6 NIV emphasis added). "Go into your room" suggests that you need to stop what you are doing and find a place that affords you privacy, mentally or physically, to meet with God. "Close the door" moves you to a place of additional privacy. Closing the door is how you sound-proof your mind from the externals of life. When I was a student of Speech-language pathology and Audiology at Columbia University one of my first clinical tasks was to be the "assigned patient" for a hearing test. In order to shut out competing signals from the environment, I had to sit in a sound-proofed testing booth.

"Prayer not only brings power into our lives, it also brings broken- ness. The Cross must break all our opinions, our willful actions. . .our self-love – our all."

Ron Halvorsen

The Secret Prayer

It was uncanny; the only sound I heard before that of the person speaking through the microphone was my own heartbeat. Imagine finding a quiet place where the only voice you can hear is that of God speaking to your heart! Isaiah confirms this type of privacy when he says "Come, my people, enter thou into thy chambers, and shut the doors about thee. . . ." (Isaiah 26:20). Here is an offering of the safety and security that can only be found in that locked-in experience with God! There you are free to tell Him your most hidden secrets and fears then He in turn brings comfort to your soul that completely eradicates every burden.

The Secret Prayer

Jesus invites us to a place of solace. Solace is what one seeks when in need of comfort. Solace is our Sanctuary! A sanctuary is a shelter – a port in the storm! A safe haven. No wonder the song writer declares:

"The Lord's our rock

In Him we hide. . .

The raging storms may

round us beat

A shelter in the time of storm

We'll never leave our safe

retreat. . .

A shelter in the time of

storm. . . ."

In the secret space of anointing

The Secret Prayer

"It is in the secret prayer space that we receive the full affirmation of the Holy Spirit."

The secret prayer space is exactly where the Holy Spirit finds us. He is the One who brings about a renewal of our nature with His anointing. He gives us that authority to go forth, and intercede on the behalf of others. The paradox of the secret prayer experience is that revelation happens! It is in this holy space that God privately and publicly transforms our lives! It is in the secret prayer space that we receive the full affirmation of the Holy Spirit. Jesus the Anointed One made the provision that we too can become anointed through the power of the Holy Spirit living in us.

The Holy Spirit's presence is not necessarily demonstrated by

"When we step into the presence of God, we are exposing ourselves to eternally powerful forces. Everything within us changes when we touch the radiating glory that emits from His face."

Bob Sorge

The Secret Prayer

outward physical histrionics, but by a changed life that is constantly seeking communion with God. Our anointing is manifested in our daily walk with Him. It is demonstrated in our desire to share Him with others. It is proclaimed in how we respond in times of trouble. Our anointing lies in the confidence we have that ". . .in the time of trouble he shall hide me in his pavilion: in the secret of his tabernacle shall he hide me; he shall set me up upon a rock." (Psalm 27: 5).

In the secret place with God, we receive power. Jesus while here on earth received the anointing from God through His daily secret pray life. In Acts 10:38 Peter announces

The Secret Prayer

"In that secret place with God, we can receive a refreshing experience and an anointing that gives evidence of His presence in our lives."

". . .God anointed Jesus of Nazareth with the Holy Ghost and with power: who went about doing good, and healing all that were oppressed of the devil; for God was with him." So we too can experience that same power when we set aside time from the banal experiences of life to seek God's face. In that secret place with God, we can receive a refreshing experience and an anointing that gives evidence of His presence in our lives.

The question now is what does the anointing look like in your life? It has to mean more than the symbolic application of oil on the forehead. The reality is that anointing comes only from the Holy Spirit. Isaiah clearly

"Talking to men for God is a great thing, but talking to God for men is greater still."

E. M. Bounds

The Secret Prayer

supports this thought when he says, "The Spirit of the Lord God is upon me; because the Lord has anointed me to preach good tidings unto the meek; he hath sent me to bind up the brokenhearted, to proclaim liberty to the captives, and the opening of the prison to them that are bound;" (Isaiah 61:1). Isaiah for one thing responded to God's call. Obviously he had to be in a place where he could hear and recognize the voice of God. That is the place of prayer! Once he heard the voice of God, he then responded. This says to me that a person has to be willing and receptive to God's voice. Having satisfied those requirements, then God reveals the particulars of

The Secret Prayer

"Our obedient response to the voice of God is the proof of our anointing, an experience that can only be obtained when we enter into that secret place with Him."

the anointing: speaking a timely word or ministering to the specific need of another. Our obedient response to the voice of God is the proof of our anointing, an experience that can only be obtained when we enter into that secret place with Him. This anointing brings power to overcome every temptation just as Christ did.

People often question the possibility of successfully overcoming temptations just as Christ did, after all He was God. Jesus came to earth as a human being. He did not use His divine ability to do any of the things He asked us to do. He led His disciples by precept and example. His precept was to be totally dependent upon His

"Prayer will make a man cease from sin, or sin will entice a man to cease from prayer."

John Bunyan

The Secret Prayer

"His precept was to be totally dependent upon His Heavenly Father. His example was to make daily prayer his bolster."

Heavenly Father. His example was to make daily prayer his bolster. The Bible tells us that as a man, He ". . . .was in all points tempted like as we are, yet without sin." (Hebrews 4: 15).

"Because he was human, Jesus had to rely on His Heavenly father for strength and power. Jesus revealed no qualities, and exercised no powers, that men may not have through faith in Him. His perfect humanity is that which all His followers may possess, if they will be in subjection to God as He was."[4]

To be successful in overcoming temptation we have to apply the same

> *"Four things let us ever keep: God hears prayer, God heeds prayer, God answers prayer, and God delivers by prayer."*
>
> *E. M. Bounds*

The Secret Prayer

"Because He was human, Jesus had to rely on His Heavenly father for strength and power."

principles Christ did. He attributed all of His strength and power to His Father. In fact, He said, "I can of mine own self do nothing. . . ." (John 5:30). His own admission speaks to His total reliance on His Father. Christ came to this earth to show humanity that it was possible for the first Adam to live a perfectly sinless life through obedience. In other words, He, as the second Adam had to be successful where the first Adam failed. Since we are born in sin and shaped in iniquity, it does appear that the odds are stacked against us. But the Bible tells us that in order for us to be able to overcome sin, we ". . .must be born again." (John 3:7). It is by way of this

The Secret Prayer

spiritual rebirth and the righteousness of Christ that we can successfully overcome every besetting sin. Daily, we can achieve this goal as we learn to seek power from God through secret communion with Him.

1. E.G. White. *Testimonies for the Church* 2: 189,190

2 .E.G. White *Desire of Ages*, p.6641 3

3. E. G. White. *The Youth's Instructor*, April, 1883.

4. E.G. White. *Desire of Ages*. 362,363

5. T. Austin-Sparks. *The Anointing of the Holy Ghost*. 2012. Online Library Austin-Sparks.Net5.

6. M. Saunders. *Come with me to the Secret Place: The Place to find Solace*

"*In prayer it is better to have a heart without words than words without a heart.*"

John Bunyan

4

THE WORDLESS PRAYER

"There is a mighty power in prayer. . .An appeal to heaven by the humblest saint is more to be dreaded by Satan than the decrees of cabinets or the mandates of kings."[1]

The story of Hannah in the Bible is a powerful authentication of the "mighty power in prayer" from the heart of the humblest suppliant. Hannah was emotionally distraught! She had been humiliated, teased and

The Wordless Prayer

"The emotionality of her heart was so utterly excruciating that it rendered her completely voiceless."

taunted by her husband's second wife, who was able to produce children by him while she, Hannah, could not. The daily insults mollified her beyond words. In fact, this is the state in which we find Hannah as we pick up her story in 1 Samuel 1: 12, 13. The emotionality of her heart was so utterly excruciating that it rendered her completely voiceless. Voice specialists today would, in all likelihood, diagnose her with a disorder known as "Functional Dysphonia." A condition in which the vocal mechanism is healthy but the individual is unable to produce any voice. This state can be induced by high emotional stress or some traumatic experience. So here

"In the silence of the heart God speaks. If you face God in prayer and silence, God will speak to you."

Mother Teresa

The Wordless Prayer

was Hannah, unable to function in the one role for which she no doubt felt divinely called as a woman – to have a child - and to make matters worse, her arch enemy, her husband's other wife was able to produce not one child but several children. This state of affairs weighed heavily on her emotional system. Consequently, in this vulnerable state, Hannah is driven to her knees. So we find her in the temple praying, but unable to lend vocal expressions to her prayer. *"As she kept on praying to the Lord. . .her lips were moving but her voice was not heard. . ."* (1 Samuel 1:12, 13 NIV emphasis added). Such intense agony

The Wordless Prayer

"When life caves in on you and grief strikes with utter intensity, you do not need to struggle for words, be assured that God is a keen Listener to these wordless prayers."

transcended the eloquence of words, but God listened to the anguish of her soul.

When life caves in on you and grief strikes with utter intensity, you do not need to struggle for words, be assured that God is a keen Listener to these wordless prayers. One phenomenon of human communication is that much information is transmitted wordlessly compared to that via speech. When you are close to someone, it is not unusual to sense their feelings without an expressed word. If this can happen between mere individuals, it should come as no surprise, that God is able to read your wordless prayers as well!

> *"Tell Jesus your wants in the sincerity of your soul. You are not required to hold a long controversy with, or preach a sermon to God. . . ."*
>
> *E. G. White*

The Wordless Prayer

"It was not that I doubted God's presence, I just couldn't find the words to utter a prayer. Somehow in my anger, anxiety and grief, I just knew He heard my soul."

Sylvia came home from work one evening to discover that after seventeen years of marriage, her husband had simply walked out on her. Only a short note meticulously penned, said, *"Goodbye. Tell the kids it's not their fault."* What could she do! Overcome with grief, her lips could not form the words to call out to God in prayer. Sylvia sat on the sofa with her knees hunched up to her chin. She rocked herself back and forth desperately attempting to make sense of the situation. Years later Sylvia recalled, "It was not that I doubted God's presence, I just couldn't find the words to

"Teach me how to quiet my racing, rising heart So I might hear the answer You are Trying to impart."

Helen Steiner Rice

The Wordless Prayer

utter a prayer. Somehow in my anger, anxiety and grief, I just knew He heard my soul."

God created us as emotional beings, and He certainly is aware that there are times when we fail at mastering our emotions. But in His great love and mercy He has provided His Holy spirit who "works upon our hearts, drawing out prayers and penitence."[2] In other words, the Holy Spirit reads our moods; when we are distraught, hurt, lonely, or grieved He translates these feelings into prayers which He then presents to God on our behalf. Paul very clearly makes this fact known to us. *"In the same way, the Spirit helps us in our weakness.*

The Wordless Prayer

We do not know what we ought to pray for, but the Spirit himself intercedes for us through wordless groans" (Romans 8: 26 NIV emphasis added).

Not all wordless prayers are born out of negative experiences. Think back to the many occasions when you were stunned by God's goodness and mercy; perhaps you received an unexpected promotion on your job, or a check in the mail! Laughter or tears of joy may have been your first response, but even then your heart was thanking and praising God. This is what I call the soul-prayer! A wordless prayer! And here is how the Holy Spirit works as our mediator:

The Wordless Prayer

"It is vital that we maintain our connection with God regardless of the surge of human emotions we may be experiencing."

"He works on our hearts, drawing out. . .praise and thanksgiving. The gratitude which flows from our lips is the result of the Spirit striking the cords of the soul in holy memories. . . ."[3]

It is vital that we maintain our connection with God regardless of the surge of human emotions we may be experiencing. A constant open pathway to heaven guarantees the presence of the Holy Spirit as the ever abiding Translator of the pleas from the soul.

I watched the wordless expressions of joy on the face of the mother of sixteen year Olympian gymnast Gabby Douglas who won a gold medal

> *"Each time before you intercede, be quiet first, and worship God in His Glory."*
>
> *Andrew Murray*

The Wordless Prayer

"There is an undeniable purity in the wordless prayer. It is simply giving God the contents of the soul without the pretentious wrappings of words!"

for the USA. She, (the mother) was speechless! One did not have to hear words from her lips! The endless pride and joy was splashed all over her face. The expressions of heart did not require words. The whole world saw that! Is there any wonder that our Father can read the wordless prayer of a grateful heart?

There is an undeniable purity in the wordless prayer. It is simply giving God the contents of the soul without the pretentious wrappings of words! The wordless prayer is one of the purest forms of communicating with God. I was driving along a strip of highway one day and was literally awestruck by the majestic beauty of

"In times of sudden difficulty or peril the heart may send up its cry for help to One who has pledged Himself to come to the aid of His faithful."

E. G. White

The Wordless Prayer

the rolling mountains, the gently sloping hills with their various hues of green. I was lost for words. I pulled over, took a deep breath in the midst of my speechlessness. In the moment of that experience I knew I was praising God for the beauty of the earth. But I had no words! I was overpowered by a great awareness that any word I uttered during that moment of awe would have failed to capture the beauty of the visual experience. Such is the prayer of the soul!

I like to think of the wordless prayer as a place, whether physical or mental, where I can retreat to allow my mind to connect with God. It is a level of connection that supersedes

The Wordless Prayer

"A bonus derived from the wordless prayer is that it allows you to hear the voice of God more clearly. It cocoons you in an atmosphere where you can escape from the clamor and clutter of life and hear the "still small voice" of God."

any type of vocalization. It is a place to which one can retire after the din and chaos of daily activities. Have you ever tried to say something to someone but your words failed to convey your message adequately? You know in your heart what you want to say and for the life of you the words don't seem to match up to what you are thinking! The wordless prayer bypasses this faulty system and allows your soul to speak frankly. A bonus derived from the wordless prayer is that it allows you to hear the voice of God more clearly. It cocoons you in an atmosphere where you can escape from the clamor and clutter of life and hear the "still small voice"

The Wordless Prayer

of God. The words of an old hymn comes to mind right now:

"There is a place of quiet rest,

Near to the heart of God,

A place where sin cannot molest,

Near to the heart of God.

O Jesus blest Redeemer,

Sent from the heart of God,

Hold us, who wait before Thee,

Near to the heart of God."

1 SDA Bible Commentary, vol.2, 1008

2 E.G. White Manuscript 50, 1900

3 Ibid.

"[The Lord] reaches deeper into our lives. He hears and answers our needs before we even ask."

Richard P. Carlson

5

The Prayer of Praise

THE PRAYER OF PRAISE

"The prayer of praise and adoration is the highest form of prayer in that this type of prayer asks nothing from God, but simply allows you to offer expressions of His ever abiding goodness."

The prayer of praise and adoration is the highest form of prayer in that this type of prayer asks nothing from God, but simply allows you to offer expressions of His ever abiding goodness. It might even be proper to say here that s is the single task of the angels in heaven. We are told that in angelic sequence and synchrony there is no pause as they cry out "Holy, Holy, Holy." David must have felt this when he uttered *"Lord, our Lord, how majestic is your name*

"Be careful for nothing; but in everything by prayer and supplication with thanksgiving let your requests be made known unto God."

Philippians 4:9

**The Prayer
of Praise**

in all the earth!" (Psalm 8:1 NIV emphasis added). These expressions of adoration and praise continue throughout his songs. *"I will give thanks to you, Lord, with all my heart; I will tell of all your wonderful deeds"* (Psalm 9:1 NIV emphasis added); *"I will extol the Lord at all times: His praise will always be on my lips"* (Psalm 34:1 NIV emphasis added); *"Praise our God, all peoples, let the sound of His praise be heard."* (Psalm 66:8 NIV emphasis added). So why is it necessary to praise God? David clearly knew the answer to this question. He knew that the reciprocal effect was God's full blessing over his life. Praising God has the double

**The Prayer
of Praise**

*". . .the Praise
Prayer helps to rid
us of the "give-
me-this-I-want-
that" nature of our
prayers, and places
us in an atmosphere
of "self-denying!"*

effect or maybe triple effect of removing confusion and restoring spiritual clarity. Why would a sovereign God need the praise of puny humanity? Well it turns out that in praising God, we are granted the opportunity of experiencing His tender, loving kindness towards us. There are three very important truths about the "Praise Prayer."

First, the Praise Prayer helps to rid us of the "give-me-this-I-want-that" nature of our prayers, and places us in an atmosphere of "self-denying!" I heard a preacher praying one day and his prayer was: "Lord I bless you this day. You are awesome! You are God all by Yourself and I just want to

"I will bless the LORD at all times; His praise shall continually be in my mouth. My soul will make its boast in the LORD; the humble will hear it and rejoice. O magnify the LORD with me, And let us exalt His name together."

Psalm 34: 1-4

**The Prayer
of Praise**

praise Your Holy name! You are Holy, Holy, Lord, You are Holy! I praise Your Name! Glory to You my Father, and to My Savior Jesus Christ and to the Holy Spirit! Hallelujah! Amen!" There was silence following this prayer, then in one accord the congregation picked up the praise strain and shouted "Hallelujah! Hallelujah! Hallelujah! Amen!" Wow! What an outpouring of adoration to God! The nature of the praise prayer is such that it has a positive captivating effect on those who are present. This type of prayer is beautifully captured in Psalm 150. When you have time sit and read the whole chapter. Every verse sets out an echo of praise and

The Prayer of Praise

worship to God. It epitomizes the hilt of praise. Imagine the glorious scene as the Psalmist's voice echoes through the plains of Judea: "Let everything that hath breath praise the LORD. Praise the Lord." (Psalm 150:6). In this frame of mind all self is pushed aside! All selfish ambitions and desires are rendered completely meaningless.

Secondly, the "Praise Prayer" allows us to step outside of self and unabashedly pay tribute to the Creator of all things. It is the time when we imitate the angelic host of heaven and offer joyful tribute to the King of kings! In fact, this is exactly why we were created in the first place – to

**The Prayer
of Praise**

*". . .when we utter
the "Praise Prayer"
we are in dress re-
hearsal for eternity
where we shall be
forever praising God
with all of the holy
angels."*

glorify God! This is what the angels do continuously, "Holy, holy, holy, is the LORD of hosts: the earth is full of His glory." (Isa. 6:3). The angels who have never sinned are consumed with reverence and awe just to be in the presence of God. They are forever praising His name.

"Their praise and glory are for the Lord of Hosts, who is high and lifted up. . . . As they see the future, when the whole earth shall be filled with His glory, the triumphant song of praise is echoed from one to the other."[1]

So when we utter the "Praise Prayer" we are in dress rehearsal for

> *"By Him therefore let us offer the sacrifice of praise to God continually, that is, the fruit of our lips giving thanks to His name."*
>
> *Heb. 13:15*

**The Prayer
of Praise**

eternity where we shall be forever praising God with all of the holy angels. In eternity we will no longer have to ask forgiveness of sins, or offer petitions of intercessions for others, neither will there be prayers for healing nor for relief from all of the human ailments that we now suffer because these former things would have passed away. In fact, there will be one Praise! Our utterances will be of perpetual praise to God! This fact calls for a shout of praise right now!

I must admit that I did not always understand uninhibited shouts of "hallelujahs" and other catchy spontaneous clips that people uttered in their ejaculatory praise during the

The Prayer of Praise

preached word. It seemed like such an undignified way to respond to the word of God! But one day I experienced an awakening that I shall never forget! I was at a leadership training conference. During the testimonial period one lady shared how God had miraculously delivered her from suicide. She was at a low ebb in her circumstances. The pain of living was too much for her to endure. With her mind made up she attempted to swallow the potion she'd concocted. Three times she made the attempts to end her life, but it did not happen. Not because of her fear of following through but because a power outside of herself stayed her hand on each attempt. According to this woman, ever since that experience she never ceased to praise God for intervening in what would have been a most tragic loss. Her life has been a series of total blessings to many other individuals in a ministry that now stretches across many countries.

To listen to the genuine praise that flowed from her lips and not be moved to praise God unabashedly was an impossibility. In that meeting, I found myself lifting my hands and heart in praise to the One and only God who covers us unsparingly with His mercies! I was praising God with tears streaming down my cheeks! Wow! It was right there, that

**The Prayer
of Praise**

*"I realized that for
years I had been
stifling my praise to
God because I was
concerned about
what people would
think of me in this
"free flowing state"
of praise."*

I realized a tremendous weight had been lifted from me. I prayed and praised God aloud. I realized that for years I had been stifling my praise to God because I was concerned about what people would think of me in this "free flowing state" of praise. But all praise be to the Author of Praise! I now realize that there is a heavenly derived freedom in praising God that no man can legislate, because it comes from within. It receives its impetus from a deep personal encounter with the Holy Spirit. God accepts genuine uninhibited praise! Hallelujah!

Thirdly, the "Praise Prayer" is much more than an eloquent arrangement of superfluous nouns and

I will bless the LORD at all times; His praise shall continually be in my mouth. My soul shall make her boast in the LORD: The humble shall hear thereof, and be glad. O magnify the LORD with me, and let us exalt His name together.

Psalm 34:1-3

The Prayer of Praise

adjectives aimed at God. The Praise prayer is a manifestation of the Christian's lifestyle. It is an act of worship that transcends the very walls of the church. As Billy Graham succinctly puts it "the highest form of worship is the worship of unselfish Christian service. The greatest form of praise is the sound of consecrated feet seeking out the lost and helpless."[2] This suggests that the Praise Prayer is much more than lip-service. It is expressed in service for others. It is expressed in leading someone to accept Jesus Christ as their Savior.

The Praise Prayer lifestyle is achieved through what I call the "Prayer Process Model." At the

142

The Prayer of Praise

"Your praise to God should have an intoxicating effect on others!"

expense of being generic, consider the expression "prayer changes things!" What is the process here? To reach a "praise prayer" lifestyle, you must experience a change! How? First, confession of sins. Then the forsaking of sin must follow. Next comes a life of transparency – Christ must be the visual in your life. Satan now has to shudder once your victory flag is raised. The logical sequelae is a lifestyle that emanates nothing but praise to God for the change that has come over your life. That is the process!

Your praise to God should have an intoxicating effect on others! It should make a mark on their lives. Note that I said your praise "to God!"

The Prayer of Praise

If your praise is to God, then you are automatically whited out of the picture. God will be the focus.

I like Ron Halvorsen's description of the person praising God: "Let the stream of your rejoicing leap up to heaven in fountains of enthusiasm. Let it fall to earth again in showers of beneficence. Let it fill the basin of your daily life and run over into the lives of others. Let it spill over them in a cataract of glittering joy – and then flow on." [3]

Finally, the words of Psalm 111:1 (NIV emphasis added) will receive expression in the entire life: "*I will extol the Lord with all my heart, in the council of the upright, and in the*

**The Prayer
of Praise**

assembly." The entire life is one that is fully dedicated to serving God. Recall that the angels in heaven continuously perform the singular act of service to God through Praise.

1 E.G. White, The Advent Review and Sabbath Herald, Oct 16, 1888

2 http://www.brainyquote.com/quotes/quotes/b/billygraha401823.html

3 Ron Halvorsen, Prayer Warriors, p. 96. 1995

Lord, our Lord, how majestic is your name in all the earth!

Psalm 8:9 NIV

6

THE INTERCESSORY PRAYER

“*My intercessor is my friend as my eyes pour out tears to God; on behalf of a man he pleads with God as one pleads for a friend.*” (Job 16: 20, 21 NIV emphasis added). Job knew what it was like to be in need of someone to intercede for him. He clearly understood the nature of the intercessory prayer. One day without warning, Job found himself in a state of extreme loss. All in the space of twenty-four

147

"All Job needed at this low point in his life was for someone to call out to God on his behalf."

hours, he lost his entire worldly assets including all of his children. He had fallen into the deepest chasm of human calamity! In this place of utter disaster, he found himself devoid of a human friend willing to intercede to God on his behalf. All Job needed at this low point in his life was for someone to call out to God on his behalf. It's not that Job was afraid of God, no not at all! But in the human state of deep grief and pain, who does not want a sympathizer? Job was in a state of brokenness that defied human explanation. He was in a place where a word of comfort, a word of compassion or a word of understanding would have been a most soothing balm. The

"In calling God our Father, we recognize all His children as our brethren, all members of one. We are all a part of the great web of humanity, all members of one family. In our petitions we are to include our neighbors. . . .No one prays aright who seeks a blessing for himself alone."

E. G. White

Intercessory Prayer

best offer his wife could muster up in her own grief and turmoil was a contemptuous ". . . .Curse God and die. . ." (Job 2: 9). But he knew full well that her suggestion was far from adequate. Job's so called friends came by, and sat around without even offering to dab his wounds, or to speak to Jehovah on his behalf, but instead, they remained speechless for days! What comforters they were!

The interesting paradox of Job's story is that at the very time of his loss he was found in a place interceding to God for his children. It does not appear as if this was a one-time behavior on Job's part. One gets the impression that this patriarch was

Intercessory Prayer

"This is what godly parents do! They perpetually intercede for their children."

constantly contending with God for his sons and daughters. On this day in question, his children were partying together; it may have been a birthday party. Nothing wrong there! But Job not out of step with the frivolity of youthfulness felt the need to pray for forgiveness of any sin or error they might have committed during their state of gaiety. This is what godly parents do! They perpetually intercede for their children. Consequently, early in the morning, Job's first thought was to intercede to God for his children: *"And it was so, when the days of their feasting were gone about, that Job sent and sanctified them, and rose up early in the morning, and offered*

151

> *"We are to ask that we may give. . . .*
> *The capacity for receiving is pre-*
> *served only by imparting."*
>
> *E.G. White*

Intercessory Prayer

burnt offerings according to the number of them all: for Job said, It may be that my sons have sinned, and cursed God in their hearts. Thus did Job continually" (Job 1: 5 emphasis added). The Bible does not offer any further details about the spiritual state of Job's children when they perished, but we are assured that during their lifetime Job continually interceded for them. Job by his patient endurance and unswerving faith in God presents a testimony of a righteous man, so we are safe in assuming that his prayers were of the intercessory nature. James declares ". . . .the effectual fervent prayer of a righteous man availeth much" (James 5:16)

153

Intercessory Prayer

"The intercessory prayer carries the tone of unselfish passion for the preservation of another."

The intercessory prayer carries the tone of unselfish passion for the preservation of another. It describes the posture of a person standing in the place of another; someone who is available to do something to assuage the destruction of another; someone who is willing to ". . .stand in the gap. . . ." (Ezekiel 22:30). This is what Christ has done and continues to do for all of us. He stands before the Father constantly interceding, pleading His blood for all mankind, in the manner of the Old Testament priests. He stands as the only mediator between God the Father and sinful humanity. His remarkable intercession was dramatically displayed before the entire

Earnest intercession will be sure to bring love with it. I do not believe you can hate a man for whom you habitually pray. If you dislike any brother Christian, pray for him doubly, not only for his sake, but for your own, that you may be cured of prejudice and saved from all unkind feeling."

Charles Spurgeon

Intercessory Prayer

"It took a righteous person to stand between God and sinful man! This tells me that not everyone can intercede!"

universe, when He stepped forward and died on the cross in our place. This was the ultimate act of intercession.

Jesus Christ the model intercessor, created a template for us to follow as we commune with the Father. While He was on earth, He prayed for all. He prayed for the sick, the diseased, the demon possessed, His friends and His enemies. He continues to prayer for all of us today!

So how can we become true "prayer intercessors?" There are three distinct qualities that are present in the intercessor and hence in the prayer. The first quality is exemplified in Christ. It took a righteous person to stand between God and sinful man!

"There is no chasm in society that cannot be firmly and permanently bridged by intercession; there is no feud or dislike that cannot be healed by the same exercise of love."

- Charles H. Brent

Intercessory Prayer

This tells me that not everyone can intercede! Just as the priests in the Old Testament dispensation had to be right before God in order to perform the duties of the temple – as representatives of the people before God – so must be the individual who attempts to intercede to God on the behalf of another. To be right with God means there must be a personal intimate relationship with Him; in order to have this personal relationship with Him, one must be constantly in His presence. When this intimacy is established, then we are able to "make up the hedge, and stand in the gap. . . ." for some else!

Intercessory Prayer

Moses was a prime example of a man right with God and one who could boldly stand in the gap. He was able to do this because of his intimate connection with God. His connection with God was so well established, that the people of Israel urged him to speak to God on their behalf. (Exodus 20:19). They knew that he could be trusted as the mediator between God and themselves. This speaks volumes! The meaning of "intercessor" according to the Thesaurus is one who "interposes." In other words, one who steps in between parties at variance with each other. This describes one who is willing to take the brunt for another. This calls for a shout!

Intercessory Prayer

". . .a core characteristic of an intercessor is willingness to put self aside, and assert on behalf of another."

There was a time in the history of the Israelites when God would have destroyed them because of their sins, but Moses immediately jumped between God's wrath and the children of Israel. He boldly prayed "But now, please forgive their sin – but if not, then blot me out of the book you have written (Ex. 32:32 NIV). Now that is where an intercessor is willing to go every time.

Secondly, a core characteristic of an intercessor is willingness to put self aside, and assert on behalf of another. This means that the intercessor is one who is willing to give up so that another can achieve. So often we think of intercessory prayer

"No man can do me a truer kindness in this world than to pray for me."

Charles Spurgeon

Intercessory Prayer

"...the intercessor is one who gives up a blessing for another"

as praying for the sick, or the lonely or the economically deprived persons, and this is not incorrect. But the intercessor is one who gives up a blessing for another. One day a mother was astounded when she overheard her daughter's passionate request to God, "Dear God, bless my mother, and that blessing you had for me, give it to her first, Amen!" What a prayer!

The story of the young lad who gave up his five loaves and two fishes (John 6:9) is rightfully seen as an example of God's amazing providence. But there is a side to this story that is rarely if ever emphasized. Yes, it was God's providence that led the unnamed boy to be part of the crowd

> *". . . .Prayer opens the way for God Himself to do His work in us and through us. Let our chief work as God's messengers be intercession; in it we secure the presence and power of God to go with us.*
>
> *Andrew Murray*

Intercessory Prayer

that day. But one could say without fear of contest that the young lad stood in the gap for the temporal needs of thousands of people that day. Let's examine the story. Here is a large crowd. All eyes are no doubt riveted on the key note speaker – Jesus Christ. With an air of tender compassion, He verbally acknowledges the fact that the people are hungry. Now up steps a little boy who perhaps cries out, "here is my lunch you can have it!" This lad without argument gave up his blessing so that others could be blessed. That is intercession! Intercessory prayer is not a detached platitude of expressions; in fact it begins with you. The intercessor

"The gifted intercessor incessantly petitions heaven on the behalf of someone or a situation."

always gives up something for the other person.

Thirdly, the true intercessor is gifted. It is a fact that anyone can offer up a prayer for another person, but the real intercessor has an above average passion for the needs of others. The intercessor not only prays the sympathetic prayer, but because of that spirit-derived ability to connect with the heart, he or she is able to pray the empathetic prayer! That's the difference! Here are the special qualities of the gifted intercessor: (1) there is a sensitivity to the needs of others. This is the one who is constantly praying the unsolicited prayer. The gifted intercessor incessantly

"The Church has not yet touched the fringe of the possibilities of intercessory prayer. Her largest victories will be witnessed when individual Christians everywhere come to recognize their priesthood unto God and day by day give themselves unto prayer."

John R. Mott

Intercessory Prayer

petitions heaven on the behalf of someone or a situation. This is the one who may quietly draw you aside and whisper in your ear, "I'm praying for you," or "I'm impressed to pray over your situation." (2) The gifted intercessor is one who does not give up; perseverance is the hallmark of their prayer experience. I know an eighty-seven year old mother who has been praying for her son for over forty-five years. You might wonder to yourself, "why not give up on that prayer, surely if God were going to do something He would have done it by now!" Actually, this is the flint quality of the true intercessor. Their persistence is not born out of

Intercessory Prayer

a sense of fret or worry, but out of the calm assurance that God will answer in His own time, hence the importunity of the prayer. (3) The gifted intercessor moves under the promptings of the Holy Spirit. There is a sense of urgency or imminence. This is the person who is overcome by a strong sense of the need to pray for someone or some situation right away. The compulsion may be so strong that they may stop the task at hand simply to pray. Some years ago I was praying over a personal need. I had barely gotten up from my knees when the telephone rang and the voice on the other end was that of a dear elderly lady who said to me "I

Intercessory Prayer

"It is the Holy Spirit that leads you to a place of intercession."

was just moved to pray for you. I had to stop what I was doing to call you." She identified the very situation for which I was praying, and I knew she had no prior knowledge because I had not discussed the matter with anyone. That's the gift of intercession!

It is the Holy Spirit that leads you to a place of intercession. I have discovered that when you pray for another person's known circumstance the Holy Spirit will often lead you to intercede for more specific needs of that individual. You will identify the need in prayer in such a manner that only the Holy Spirit could have given you the information. According to Ron Halversen[1] *"when we hold others*

"It is in the field of prayer that life's critical battles are lost or won. . .In prayer we bring our spiritual enemies into the Presence of God and we fight them there."

John Henry Jowett

Intercessory Prayer

up before God, when we expose them to God's love. . . .Only then do we sense what it means to share in God's work and concerns." But I think the greatest manifestation of intercessory prayer comes straight from Jesus on the cross when He uttered "Father, forgive them; for they know not what they do."(Luke 23:34).

". . .the greatest manifestation of intercessory prayer comes straight from Jesus. . . ."

1. Ron Halvorsen. *Prayer Warriors* p.100. 1995.

"Our prayers may be awkward. Our attempts may be feeble. But since the power of prayer is in the One who hears it and not in the one who says it, our prayers do make a difference."

Max Lucado

7

PRAYING IN THE SPIRIT

There is much theological debate and controversy about praying in the spirit, a discussion which is clearly beyond the scope of this chapter. But from a lay-person's perspective, I think of the biblical expression "praying in the Spirit" as synonymous with being "moved by the Spirit" to action. If a person is moved by the Holy Spirit to pray, then the Spirit is capable enough of providing that person with the appropriate words and expressions. Praying

Praying in the Spirit

"We are totally dependent on the Holy Spirit to place the thought of praying in our minds."

in the Spirit in its simplest expression is descriptive of the individual who is led by the Spirit of God to intercede on the behalf of another. On our own, we really do not know how to pray or what to pray for. We are totally dependent on the Holy Spirit to place the thought of praying in our minds. We do not have the appropriate vocabulary, consequently He gives us the utterance. We do not have clarity on the situation that requires our intercession, therefore we need Him to identify the areas in need. Only a completely God-dependent individual can pray in the Spirit!

How can you tell that it is the Holy Spirit leading and not your own

"Any concern too small to be turned into a prayer is too small to be made into a burden."

Corrie Ten Boom

Praying in the Spirit

"The enemy cannot and will not prompt the child of God to pray. It is counterproductive to his cause to do so for it would be 'fighting against himself!'"

curious inquisitive imagination? According to Stormie Omartian, *"the Holy spirit will always lead us to pray. . .It is His will that we pray."*[1] Anytime you are prompted to pray it is the Spirit of God that is leading. I will add here that "praying ground" is restricted territory for Satan! The enemy cannot and will not prompt the child of God to pray. It is counterproductive to his cause to do so for it would be "fighting against himself!" The command to pray comes to us directly from God therefore we are on safe ground when we pray. ". . .men ought always to pray, and not faint." (Luke 18:1). You will know that you are praying in the Spirit when you

176

"When we pray for the Spirit's help . . . we will simply fall down at the Lord's feet in our weakness. There we will find the victory and power that comes from His love."

Andrew Murray

Praying in the Spirit

feel compelled to pray about the needs of others. It could be about a family member, a friend or even a total stranger. One day the telephone in my office rang. I recognized the voice of the person on the other end even though we had never met face to face. I knew the voice because periodically we worked closely via telephone. This day in particular when she called, something impressed me that she needed prayer. I had no idea whether she was a woman of faith (I discovered later that she was). I said to her "I just have an overwhelming urge to pray for you." Without verbally responding, she convulsed in uncontrollable waves of sobs. She

> ### Praying in the Spirit

> *"The Holy Spirit also places the correct words and sequences of words in our prayers . . . ."*

finally composed herself to say, "My twelve year old nephew that I'm raising as my own son, has just been diagnosed with a rare disease that can affect his heart. Yes, I am a woman of faith and yes, I do need pray. Please pray for my nephew." Prior to this phone conversation, I'd no idea what was going on in this lady's life. But I knew the Holy Spirit led me to pray for her. The Holy Spirit also places the correct words and sequences of words in our prayers, because left to ourselves, we really would not know what to pray for or how to formulate the words. "*. . .the Spirit helps us in our weakness. We do not know what we ought to pray for, but the Spirit*

179

Pray in the Spirit on all occasions with all kinds of prayers and requests. With this in mind, be alert and always keep on praying for all the saints.''

Ephesians 6:18

himself intercedes for us through wordless groans." (Romans 8:26 NIV emphasis added).

Sometimes a person with whom you have not had contact in years may suddenly pop into your mind. I have to admit that before I understood what praying in the Spirit meant, I would be dismissive of these "pop-ups" simply thinking to myself, "Hmm where did that come from?" This is especially true, if the person happens to be someone with whom you might have had a difficulty in the past, and who may now be on your "enemy-list" or "avoid-a- all-cost-list." Now if it's a good friend or a loved one that suddenly came to

Praying in the Spirit

"You will know you are praying in the Spirit when you have this uncomfortable and unquenchable urge to pray for your enemies!"

mind, you may be more prone to call them and say "Hi, how are you, I just thought of you and I could not resist checking on you!" But let's be honest right here, how comfortable are you with the idea of praying a blessing over your worst enemy? Now that's not an easily embraceable notion! Why would the Holy Spirit ask you to do such a thing?

You will know you are praying in the Spirit when you have this uncomfortable and unquenchable urge to pray for your enemies! Wow! You say well that is easy. I don't mind praying for the destruction of my enemies at all. Didn't David asked God many times to kill and destroy his enemies?

"Prayer is a sincere, sensible, affectionate pouring out of the soul to God, through Christ, in the strength and assistance of the Spirit, for such things as God has promised."

John Bunyan

Praying in the Spirit

But how about praying for the success of your worst enemy - the one who betrayed you; the one who manipulated the situation so that you were over-looked for that promotion; or the one you blamed for your unhappy marriage? If the Bible verse that says *"But I say unto you, Love your enemies, bless them that curse you, do good to them that hate you, and pray for them which despitefully use you, and persecute you;"* (Matthew 5:44 emphasis added) mean anything to you, you will be convinced that praying for your enemies is a biblically supported injunction. When you are under compulsion to pray for your enemies, you can know without doubt that you are being led by the Holy Spirit.

Finally, to pray in the Spirit means that the Holy Spirit is united with us in prayer. He partners with us. He impresses our minds. He utters through our lips and escorts us into the very presence of God!

8

GOD HEARS
EVERY PRAYER

*God has a "divine
yes" to all of our
prayers."*

We are all familiar with the saying that God answers prayers with either" yes," "no" or "wait." I don't disagree with this notion, but I see it from a different perspective. I believe that God has a "divine yes" to all of our prayers. In reality what we may perceive as His "no" is actually, through His omniscience, His "divine yes." Since He knows what's best for us, His answer must always work out for our good. That's an absolute. Because we do not

"Because He bends down to listen, I will pray as long as I have breath!"

Psalm 116: 2 NLT

**God Hears
Every Prayer**

see as He does, we are limited in our ability to discern; hence the key to this truth lies in our willingness to always trust His answer to be the best. If we do, the outcome is going to be a guaranteed positive and that, is the "Divine Yes."

The question often asked is, does God hear every prayer? Well first, what do you mean by "hear"? Given the fact that He is omniscient, all knowing, then nothing escapes His knowledge. He knows everything! So yes, He hears all prayers. If the implication of the question is does He ignore some prayers, then we will have to apply the elements of our argument discussed above about how

*God Hears
Every Prayer*

God responds. We perceive God's response to our prayers as either, "yes," "no," or "wait," and then we fashion our attitudes based on these types of responses.

Let's look at the "yes" aspect of God's response. When we present our requests to God, we expect that He will respond for the most part in the positive as we humans under-stand it, and that means a "yes." Our reciprocal response is to offer praise and gratitude and appreciation (well usually). If we do not receive the desired response within our "pre-formed" time-frame of when we think God should respond, we interpret that "silence" as a "no." Our

*God Hears
Every Prayer*

*". . .we cannot pre-
sume that we know
how God thinks. His
ways are not our
ways."*

natural reaction to our perceived "no" response is to feel, hurt, disappointed, angry, unhappy, depressed and much more. Now here lies the big problem. What does the perceived "no" from God suggest to you? Well you may say, "Perhaps He doesn't want me to have it," "He thinks I don't deserve it," or "He thinks I would be ungrateful if He grants my request." Well a lot is wrong with this line of "thinking." For one thing, we cannot presume that we know how God thinks. His ways are not our ways. *"For my thoughts are not your thoughts, neither are your ways my ways," declares the Lord. As the heavens are higher than the earth, so are my ways higher than your ways*

"May my prayer be set before you like incense; may the lifting up of my hands be like the evening sacrifice."

Psalm 141:2 NIV

God Hears Every Prayer

and my thoughts than your thoughts."(Isaiah 55:8,9 NIV emphasis added). God knows that of ourselves we can do nothing to deserve His goodness, so He does not use the measure of "deserving" to weigh His goodness towards us. He loves us unconditionally, "For God so loved the world that He gave His only begotten Son that whosoever believeth on Him should not perish but have eternal life." (John 3: 16). If we feel God is withholding our request because He knows we may not be grateful to Him, well here's an amazing fact; God does not need to use that kind of leverage with us because we have been ungrateful to

192

God Hears Every Prayer

"He already knows what is best for us. He simply invites us to trust and wait patiently on Him."

Him from the beginning, and it was for that very reason that He came to redeem us: *"But God demonstrates His own love for us in this: while we were still sinners Christ died for us."* (Romans 5:8 emphasis added). So you see we have no argument to put forward that would suggest God's response to our prayers is intrinsically based on anything we may do or an attitude we may have towards Him at the time. He already knows what is best for us. He simply invites us to trust and wait patiently on Him.

The recognition of the "wait" response is different for each one of us depending on our prayer experience with God. Some years ago,

"Revival will come when we get the walls down between the church and the community."

Jack Graham

God Hears Every Prayer

"The reality is that the Holy Spirit runs ahead of our prayers and changes the situation so that our prayers are already answered well in advance of our expectations."

I prayed for God to make a move in my career. I prayed for months and years. Sometimes my prayers waned and ceased for a while. Many years later when I was least expecting it, the career advancement I'd prayed for came. Had God answered my prayers earlier, I would not have been prepared to handle the change. All along, I had interpreted the time of His "silence" as His "no." The reality is that the Holy Spirit runs ahead of our prayers and changes the situation so that our prayers are already answered well in advance of our expectations. The "wait response" still works out to be a "divine yes!" All we have to do is to trust His wisdom.

"When we wait on God. . .we experience His goodness – we experience God Himself."

Dennis Smith

**God Hears
Every Prayer**

One very comforting fact that we must never ever gloss over lightly is the role the Holy Spirit plays in our prayers. "Likewise the Spirit also helpeth our infirmities: for we know not what we should pray for as we ought: but the Spirit itself maketh intercession for us with groanings which cannot be uttered" (Romans 8:26). This tells me very clearly that the Holy Spirit is inextricably bound up in our prayers. How? For starters, we do not know the first thing about praying to the Father, therefore, the Holy Spirit, stands in our stead. He intercedes on our behalf. Secondly, we do not know what to ask God for. We don't even know the correct

God Hears Every Prayer

thought sequence, therefore the Holy Spirit reconfigures the prayer. Given this elaborate involvement of the Holy Spirit, do you think our prayers would ever be ignored? Certainly not! Through the Holy Spirit's intercessory role, we are guaranteed a hearing! We are guaranteed a response from God that will work for our good!

So we've talked a lot about how God hears every prayer, and we've come to the conclusion that He does. Here's another question. Does God respond to all prayers or does He treat some prayers as if they were never uttered? The Word of God is very clear on conditions surrounding prayer. "If I regard iniquity in my heart, the Lord

God Hears Every Prayer

". . .if we have a feeling of respect and admiration for sin, and at the same time attempt to pray to Him, then He cannot acknowledge our prayers."

will not hear me:" (Psalm 66:18). Another word for "iniquity" is "sin." Here are two of the many definitions for the word "regard." Merriam-Webster proposes, (1) "care or concern for someone or something;" and (2) "a feeling of respect and admiration for someone or something." So God is saying through the Psalmist David, that if we have a feeling of respect and admiration for sin, and at the same time attempt to pray to Him, then He cannot acknowledge our prayers. This convergence of "sinful state" and "prayer" essentially blocks God's ability to respond. Remember He does not force His way into our lives. Furthermore, to hold sin fondly

"Waiting on God refers to the Christian's ability to maintain a confident, quiet, expectant, hopeful and peaceful trust in God at all times for all things."

Dennis Smith

God Hears Every Prayer

in the heart is to literally hold something as a god and we know that God and sin are diametrically opposed. Look at what happened to Lucifer "Thou wast perfect in thy ways from the day that thou wast created, till iniquity was found in thee." (Ezekiel 28:15). Sin caused Lucifer to be cast out of heaven from the presence of God. Sin builds walls between us and God. No wonder the prophet Isaiah says "But your iniquities have separated between you and your God, and your sins have hid his face from you that he will not hear." (Isaiah 59:2). The marvelous beauty of God's love for us is in the fact that *"If we confess our sins, He is faithful and just to*

God Hears Every Prayer

"God has promised to hear and answer every one who diligently seeks after Him. It doesn't matter, where you have been, what you have done, how old you are, your race or gender."

forgive us our sins, and to cleanse us from all unrighteousness." (1John 1: 9 emphasis added). He also promises *"All that the Father giveth me shall come to me; and him that cometh to me I will in no wise cast out."* (John 6: 37 emphasis added). God has promised to hear and answer every one who diligently seeks after Him. It doesn't matter, where you have been, what you have done, how old you are, your race or gender. He will hear the prayer of the penitent sinner and that means all of us.

> *"The prayer of faith is the great strength of the Christian and will assuredly prevail against Satan."*
>
> E. G White

9

THE PRAYER OF FORGIVENESS

I was at a Women's Retreat some years ago. On the final day of the retreat we all gathered in groups for prayer. We chose to be in groups with individuals we had either known very little about or never met before. It was hard for me because I looked around the room and I saw most people that I knew! However, there was one individual whose face was new to me, so I linked up with her and a few others. In our group we exchanged contact information and within a few short

The Prayer of Forgiveness

moments, we were all very well acquainted. But I was drawn to the woman whom I'd met for the first time. Her story would forever change my prayer life. She had an only child – daughter. Immediately I felt a connection because I too am the parent of an only child – a daughter. She poured out to me the most gut-wrenching story. Her only daughter was brutally attacked raped and killed by a vicious stranger. I felt every fear, anger, hostility, and pain one could ever imagine for this lady. I looked intently in her eyes as she told the story. The kindest softest expression peered back at me as she continued. It was now one year since the tragedy.

The Prayer of Forgiveness

"She had shed every tear that could ever be manufactured within her tear ducts. She had experienced every stage of grief that had ever been identified."

She had shed every tear that could ever be manufactured within her tear ducts. She had experienced every stage of grief that had ever been identified. Ah yes, those were the normal responses to deep tragedy. I was emotionally caught up in her story. I expected to hear her say words such as, "If I ever get near that criminal, I would. . ." or "I hope he never ever sees the light of day!" I went on and on in my mind picturing the justifiable scenarios of punishment that would be appropriate for this criminal! But never in a million years did I expect to hear what this mother said next. In the court, during the closing hours of the case, she was allowed to address

> *"The prayer of forgiveness is always answered immediately. . . . God may give us something other than we ask, but not when we ask for deliverance from sin."*
>
> E. G. White

The Prayer of Forgiveness

"I want you to know that I forgive you."

the man and here's what she said: "I want you to know that I forgive you. Nothing I can say now will ever bring my daughter back. Your death cannot bring my daughter back. I am praying for you. As a mother, I have love in my heart for you!" The woman turned to the judge and said, "Your honor, I know that there is a debt to society this man must pay, but I am asking you to spare his young life." What a tale of forgiveness! When the woman concluded her story to me that morning, I stood condemned! I recognized that I had a warped notion, if any at all, about forgiveness. She stood before me as an example of what Christ on the cross meant when He said, "Father

"If we confess our sins, he is faithful and just to forgive us our sins, and to cleanse us from all unrighteousness"

1 John 1:9

The Prayer of Forgiveness

forgive them!" What this woman did for the young man was to offer him a freedom that no court in the land could offer. She granted him not only freedom from his unspeakable act but hope for a future. This is exactly what Jesus Christ came to this earth to do for the entire world. He willingly offered us pardon from all of our wrong doings. In fact He became the sin that we committed so that we could be sinless! It surely boggles the mind to attempt to grasp the nature of Christ's forgiveness of our sins. Long before it even dawned upon our finite minds that we were in need of forgiveness, He forgave us. According

> *The Prayer of Forgiveness*

"As soon as there was sin there was a Savior."

to E.G. White "As soon as there was sin, there was a Saviour."[1]

Forgiveness is bi-directional. First, there is the forgiveness that comes to us directly from God when we seek to be forgiven of our trespasses. Secondly, there is the forgiveness that we extend to those who have trespass against us. These two components of forgiveness are inextricably bound. In the Lord's Prayer, Jesus clearly states *"And forgive us our debts, as we also have forgiven our debtors." (*Matthew 6:12 NIV emphasis added*).*The principle that Jesus has set out here is the reciprocity of forgiveness: Divine forgiveness is inherently related to the forgiveness we extend to others.

"Don't be afraid to pray for others because you are concerned that your prayers might not be answered. It's your job to pray and God's job is to answer. You have to do your job and let God do His."

Stormie Omartian

The Prayer of Forgiveness

". . .if you want to be forgiven, you must be prepared to forgive. Plain and simple."

The prayer of forgiveness acknowledges that a wrong was committed and the penitent individual is now seeking to correct this wrong. In order for the correction to be made, a full acquiescence must be made about the wrong, and furthermore, the person seeking forgiveness must be opened to the idea of rendering forgiveness to anyone who has done them a wrong. In other words, if you want to be forgiven, you must forgive. Plain and simple.

Praying for forgiveness is much deeper than a generalized request "Lord forgive me of all my sins." Forgiveness requires specificity. It requires one to identify the person

"But if you do not forgive men their sins, your Father will not forgive your sins."

Matthew 6:15

The Prayer of Forgiveness

wronged and the specific wrong committed. Recall David's prayer of forgiveness recorded in Psalm 51. He identified the Person whom he wronged. "Against Thee, Thee only, have I sinned. . . ." (v.4). He acknowledged that he had committed an offense directly against God. He was emphatic – "against Thee, Thee only." Next, he pinpointed the specific action. ". . .*this* evil in thy sight:" Notice David did not say "I have done *an* evil." In the King James Version the word "this" is used as the definite article, thus identifying the particular action being referenced. The forgiveness request must be honest and transparent. The

The Prayer of Forgiveness

prayer of forgiveness leaves no room for excuses. I have discovered four fundamental elements that seem to pervade the prayer of forgiveness.

First, the individual is fully convicted that he or she has committed a wrong. Therefore there is the element of guilt. In this state of mind, the individual commences to seek out the person wronged. Notice in Psalm 51, David realized that his awful wrong doing was against God therefore he sought God, he went directly to Him. He did not go to the priest Nathan, his wrongful act had nothing to do with this priest of God. David could not go to Uriah because he had already killed him. Rather, he made his vertical

The Prayer of Forgiveness

"In seeking forgiveness one is beset by an insatiable desire to correct a wrong that was done. This sense of guilt is so strong that nothing but confession appeases the mind."

appeal to the God of heaven – "Have mercy upon me, O God. . ." (v.1). I imagine seeing David beating his breast as he repeatedly uttered these words! But first I see him torn by a guilty conscience, not daring to look up to heaven but lying face buried in the dirt! That is how low he felt! In seeking forgiveness one is beset by an insatiable desire to correct a wrong that was done. This sense of guilt is so strong that nothing but confession appeases the mind. This is what led the psalmist to cry out *"Search me, Oh God, and know my heart. . . ."* (Psalm 139:23 emphasis added). According to Ellen White[2] "the confession that is the outpouring of the inmost soul

"Forgiveness is not an occasional act, it is a constant attitude."

Martin Luther King Jr.

The Prayer of Forgiveness

". . .when we are at the point of extreme discomfort, then, God starts the process of healing that of necessity comes with forgiving!

finds its way to the God of infinite pity." This is what the psalmist is echoing when he says "The Lord is close to the brokenhearted and saves those who are crushed in Spirit." (Psalm 34:18 NIV). It is not that God takes some morbid delight in seeing us squirm in our seats! Not at all! Rather, when we are moved to a place where our sin embarrasses us, when we find ourselves guilt-ridden to such a degree that we of necessity feel inwardly broken, when we are at the point of extreme discomfort, then, God starts the process of healing that of necessity comes with forgiving!

Secondly, bound up in the prayer of forgiveness, is heart-wrenching

"If the dream you have in your heart does not in any way match the call God has on your life, surrender your dream to the Lord. If it is not of Him, He will take it away and replace it with His."

Stormie Omartian

The Prayer of
Forgiveness

sorrow for one's action. This sorrow is so deep that one is willing to seek out any means that would obliterate the wrong. No wonder David cried out from the depths of his extreme sorrow *"Purge me with hyssop, and I shall be clean: wash me and I shall be whiter than snow."* (Psalm 51:7 emphasis added). The metaphor carries with it the idea of a contamination that cannot respond to any ordinary detergent! It requires a cleansing that only God can do. According to Exodus 12:22 and Numbers 19:18 the priests often used hyssop in the purification process. It was dipped in water and sprinkled not only on all the vessels of the sanctuary but on all who were seeking

The Prayer of Forgiveness

"In his deep sorrow for his sin, David recognized that he needed someone outside of himself who had the power to "sanitize". . . him from the awful deed he had done."

forgiveness of sins. Hyssop was used in the application of the blood of the slain lamb upon the door posts. In his deep sorrow for his sin, David recognized that he needed someone outside of himself who had the power to "sanitize" or as one author says "de-sin" him from the awful deed he had done. He was willing to undergo the necessary treatment just so he could be sin-free again.

A third element around which the prayer of forgiveness reverberates is that of confession. In fact this is the core element! Remember 1 John 1:9 *"If we confess our sins, He is faithful and just to forgive us our sins, and to cleanse from all unrighteousness."*

"Whenever you stand praying, if you have anything against anyone, forgive him, that your Father in heaven may also forgive you your trespasses."

Mark 11:25 NKJV

*The Prayer of
Forgiveness*

(Emphasis added). That is so plain! Confession goes way beyond just saying "God please forgive me of my sins." It identifies the particular sin! True confession may require seeking those individuals that suffered injury from the particular wrong action -whether physical or emotional. It requires acknowledging the error that was made.

What do you do if circumstances are of such a nature that there is no way humanly possible for you to reach the person whom you have wronged? Well, this is where we take that situation to the God of heaven who ultimately grants the forgiveness. We are admonished to confess

"Trust in the fact that the blood of Jesus is far reaching enough to cover every sin."

our faults to each other but our sins to Him. This does not mean that faults are not sins! It simply means that we must seek to be in harmony with each other first, then, go to God for ultimate forgiveness of our wrong doing. But if it's not possible to locate the person wronged then seek forgiveness from heaven. Look at it like this, even when you ask the person to forgive you, there is still the ultimate forgiveness that must come from God! Trust in the fact that the blood of Jesus is far reaching enough to cover every sin. Even if the person is dead, and the Holy Spirit brings to your mind the wrong deed you did or that the person may have done to you,

". . .clothe yourselves with compassion, kindness, humility, gentleness and patience. Bear with each other and forgive one another. . . .Forgive as the Lord forgave you."

Colossians 3: 12, 13

The Prayer of Forgiveness

ask God to forgive you in the first instance, of the wrong you did, and next forgive you for not forgiving the person at the time. You will discover the immense freedom forgiveness brings!

For years I kept a grudge against an individual who had done something terrible to me, at least in my opinion, it was terrible. I felt, since I was the person wronged, that I should have been the recipient of an apology. So I kept this anger in my heart. I'd almost forgotten about it. Years later, I had a chance meeting with the individual. All the hurt from the past welled up in my heart. Clearly, the person had moved on with their life, but I was

The Prayer of Forgiveness

still held captive! More years went by. I still bore what I felt was "justifiable resentment" towards the person. But it was at a prayer conference when I was led through the prayer of forgiveness by the presenter, that I experienced freedom! I was able to recognize that I needed to forgive that person whether I had received an apology or not! I realized I was duty bound to forgive! I first had to ask God to forgive me of the years of deep resentment I felt towards the individual, then I literally uttered, "I forgive." The tremendous freedom and relief I experienced was unspeakable. That's what forgiveness will do for you.

The Prayer of Forgiveness

"The beauty of God's gift of forgiveness is that it offers us a new life, new hope and a new beginning with Him."

The fourth element of forgiveness that really clinches it, is reformation. Confession will only be acceptable to God if there is the accompanying change in behavior. Wow! This is that right about turn that God expects! Forgiveness is not just granted to us, there has to be intentional action on our part. We can expect forgiveness when we have made "decided changes in the life; everything offensive to God must be put away."[3] Turning from the specific sin is the reformative component that is contingent on the gift of forgiveness that God alone can grant.

The beauty of God's gift of forgiveness is that it offers us a new life,

"When you've experienced grace. . .you're a lot more forgiving of other people. You're a lot more gracious to others."

Rick Warren

The Prayer of Forgiveness

". . .when we confess and forsake our sins. . . .He forgives us and we have a new start."

new hope and a new beginning with Him. Imagine if a benefactor were to visit you one day and say. "All of your past debts have been cleared. You have a new start. Your credit score is perfect. All of the failing grades have been removed. All negative evaluations from your boss have been removed. Your record is clear and clean!" What a life that would be! And yet, this is exactly what God does for us when we confess and forsake our sins. He forgives us and we have a new start.

1. E.G. White. *Review* and Herald March 12, 1901

2. E.G. White. *Steps to Christ.* p.41

3. Ibid p. 42

> *"For they shall all know me, from the least of them unto the greatest of them, saith the Lord: for I will forgive their iniquity, and I will remember their sin no more."*
>
> *Jeremiah 31:34*

10

PRAYING WITH POWER

P rayer is actually much easier than we think it is. In fact it is the most easily accessible and powerful weapon available to the weakest saint. Satan knows this better than any of us, that's why he is always seeking to either distract us from prayer, quench our desire to pray or make us feel self-conscious about praying! He creates dozens of excuses in our heads as to why we should or cannot pray. I had dental work done on my upper molars. Even though the spaces

"Prayer. . .is the most easily accessible and powerful weapon available to the weakest saint."

233

"Satan will use any situation to prevent us from praying because he knows that there is unstoppable power in prayer and that power is unleashed against him!"

Violet Cox

Praying with Power

on my gum were not readily visible, I was plagued by the notion that everyone who looked at me was magnetically drawn to my missing molars! During a church service one of the pastors asked me to pray. I froze. I could not bring myself to stand before the congregation to pray! My excuse? I had missing molars! Was that pride or what? Satan will use any situation to prevent us from praying because he knows that there is unstoppable power in prayer, and that power is unleashed against him! Sadly, we often fall for his subtle schemes and miss the opportunity to tap in to God's power.

Praying with Power

"The reality is that when we pray, we are on protected and restricted territory. That scares the devil away!"

Why is it that we do not pray as much as we should? Perhaps because we don't fully understand the tremendous power we can access through prayer. The reality is that when we pray, we are on protected and restricted territory. That scares the devil away! Ellen White[1] echoes this same thought:

"The enemy cannot overcome the humble learner of Christ, the one who walks prayerfully before the Lord. Christ interposes Himself as a shelter, a retreat, from the assaults of the wicked one. . . .There is no power in the whole satanic force that can

236

> *"When we enter the realm of prayer we are actually inviting God to come into our circumstance and to meet us at the point where we are in most need."*
>
> *Violet Cox*

Praying with Power

disable the soul that trusts, in simple confidence, in the wisdom that comes from God.

When we enter the realm of prayer we are actually inviting God to come into our circumstance and to meet us at the point where we are in most need. He in turn provides us with the power to resist all kinds of temptations the enemy brings. In this place called prayer, we can never be defeated by the enemy. By the same token, prayer gives us the power to wrestle with God. This is the kind of power Jacob experienced. Why did he prevail with God? Simply put, he held on to God tenaciously all through the

Praying with Power

"It was the holding on that was essentially powerful. It is in the "holding" that the victory is won!"

night! The fact is that even though Jacob was struggling to hold on to the angel. It was God Himself, who provided Jacob with the power to keep up the fight! That is powerful! It was not solely the fact that Jacob wrestled all night long that was so powerful. But it was the fact that at the end of the fight when his strength was almost depleted, Jacob still held on to the angel. It was the "holding on," that was essentially powerful. It is in the "holding" that the victory is won! Can you imagine what would have happened if Jacob had failed to "hold on?" In his own words Jacob declared "I will not let you go unless you bless me." (Genesis 32: 26 NIV).

"Four things let us ever keep in mind: God hears prayer, God heeds prayer, God answers prayer, and God delivers by prayer."

E. M. Bounds

Praying with Power

Jacob recognized the power of God in the night long struggle. He had too much at stake to let go without a blessing. Frequently, we miss out on the blessings God has for us because we "let go of the arm of the Lord too soon."[2] We are told to press our "petitions to the throne, and hold on by strong faith."[3]

The power of the prayer is not measured by its length or eloquence of articulation. That could not be more far removed from the truth! Actually, it is the simple, sincere and honest prayer that attracts God's attention. Jesus told the story of two men praying in the temple. One was audacious and loud. He declared

Praying with Power

"Powerful prayers all seem to have a common thread – brevity! There is an element of immediacy in these types of prayers."

himself to God, no doubt in the most sanctimonious terms and postures. The other man, ashamed and embarrassed, simply clasped his chest and begged for forgiveness! According to Jesus, it was the latter who walked away justified. (Read Luke 18:9-14).

Powerful prayers all seem to have a common thread – brevity! There is an element of immediacy in these types of prayers. There is no denying the fact of Nehemiah's urgent need as he stood before the king. His prayer was so brief that it was not even measured in words, but rather, in the semibreve of time that elapsed between the king's question and his

> *"When prayer has become secondary, or incidental, it has lost its power. Those who are conspicuously men of prayer are those who use prayer as they use food, or air, or light, or money."*
>
> *M.E. Andross*

Praying with Power

response! Yet we all recognize the power of his prayer – every potential obstacle in his pathway was removed!

Among the many power-packed prayers in the Bible, I think of the prayer Jesus prayed for the deaf mute. *"Then Jesus looked up in prayer, groaned mightily, and commanded, "Ephphatha! – Open up!" And it happened. The man's hearing was clear and his speech plain – just like that."* (Mark 7:34, 35 MSG emphasis added) This was Jesus teaching us the immediacy of God's response. *"And it happened."* That's the power that takes effect upon your life when your gaze is upward and you call on Him. It's not the multiplicity of words that

Praying with Power

"In that upward gaze, there is little chance of distraction. The mind is now fully opened to God and His power can flow in."

brings about the effect but rather that upward gaze towards heaven as the heart of man meets the heart of God. Jesus' prayer posture of looking up to heaven, as so often depicted by artists, conveys a connectivity of heart to heart with God.

In that upward gaze, there is little chance of distraction. The mind is now fully opened to God and His power can flow in. Note the authority that Jesus, as a human being, held through His connection with His father. He commanded ears to hear, mouths to speak clearly and dead people to live again. This is power! In the account of the deaf mute we read in Mark 7:34-35, the power that Jesus had with

245

"This is the confidence we have in approaching God: that if we ask anything according to His will, He hears us."

1 John 5:14

Praying with Power

His Father was transferred immediately to the man's lifeless ear causing him to hear, and to his mute tongue causing speech to gush forth. That same kind of power is available to us today. In fact, greater power has been promised to us. Jesus told His disciples that they would have the capability of doing "greater" works than He did (John 14:12). This assurance has been extended to us in terms of the magnitude of influence and power we can affect today under the guidance of the Holy Spirit. Such is the power that is available to us through prayer.

1. E.G White. *My Life Today* p. 316.

2. E.G. White. *Early Writings Chapter 18, p.72*

3. Ibid

THREE POWERFUL PRAYERS

"When I think of praying with power, I immediately think of the men and women of the Bible who had the ability to arrest God's attention by their uncommon faith."

When I think of praying with power, I immediately think of the men and women of the Bible who had the ability to arrest God's attention by their uncommon faith. Who is not moved by the prayers of Elijah on Mount Caramel, Daniel in the king's palace, Moses as he interceded on behalf of the Children of Israel, Esther before the king or Naomi over her daughters-in-law? All of these are well known Bible

> *"Our prayer and God's mercy are like two buckets in a well; while one ascends, the other descends."*
>
> *Arthur Hopkins*

Three Powerful Prayers

characters who led tremendous prayer lives. But the Word of God is replete with many other "prayer giants" nevertheless, who are not often highlighted or perhaps even counted as such, yet when the fruit of their lives is examined their pathway of prayer becomes readily apparent.

Let's take another look at the familiar story of woman with the issue of blood. What a compelling account! Her bold action is well known and frequently preached about, but the power of her prayer is less highlighted. Here's a woman who was imprisoned by a disease. She had done all that she knew to do to find healing, but her efforts failed as did all of her

Three Powerful Prayers

finances. She was in a place of utter desperation. Can you imagine being at the point of your circumstance, where everything and everyone you trusted failed you, and the next sure possible outcome is death? This is exactly where this woman found herself. Recently, I heard a young woman tell her personal testimony of suffering such excruciating pain from a debilitating illness that she prayed for death! None of the doctors she had seen could help her. In desperation she turned to the internet to find a doctor anywhere in the world who might be able to offer her one last shred of hope. Through her internet searches she finally discovered one doctor

Three Powerful Prayers

"Without too much fanfare on the outside, but charged on the inside with electrifying sparks of hope, this woman prayed one of the most power packed prayers ever recorded in the Bible."

over a six hundred miles away from her home who was willing to offer her the help she needed. Desperation led this woman to travel to the unknown to find a cure, and she did! Likewise, the woman with the issue of blood desperately needed a cure. When it seemed as though all hope had taken flight, then her breakthrough came! She heard of a Man called Jesus who was going around the cities healing people and even raising the dead. Everywhere He went crowds of people followed, looking for their miracle! Without too much fanfare on the outside, but charged on the inside with electrifying sparks of hope, this woman prayed one of the most power

> *"God hears prayer, God heeds prayer, God answers prayer, and God delivers by prayer."*
>
> *E. M. Bounds*

Three Powerful Prayers

packed prayers ever recorded in the Bible. This was not a public prayer. It was not uttered aloud. In fact no one but God heard her tremendous outcry from an inner place of desperate need. ". . .*If I may but touch his garment, I shall be whole.*" (Matthew 9:20 emphasis added). The real power is in her emphatic assertion "*I shall.*" There is no hint of doubt in the literary supra-segmental she simultaneously urged upon the utterance "*shall.*" I believe it gave rise to the propulsion that catapulted her to that certain place in the crowd whereby she surreptitiously reached out or perhaps lounged forward, and touched the fringes of Jesus' garment.

"All we have to do is to make that certain connection with God that ultimately gives rise to the "supra-natural!"

All we have to do is to make that certain connection with God that ultimately gives rise to the "supra-natural!" This woman experienced her healing not so much from the touch as from her unshakeable faith in the fact that her healing was a guaranteed "fait accompli." No wonder Jesus' response to her prayer so dramatically expressed in her action was "*. . . .Your faith has healed you.*" (Matthew 9:22 NIV emphasis added).

Nestled among the historical bevy of kings of Israel that did both good and evil in the sight of God, is the story of King Asa. His reign was characterized by peace because he did the good in the sight of the lord. But

> *"...True prayer is measured by weight, not by length. A single groan before God may have more fullness of prayer in it than a fine oration of great length."*
>
> *C. H. Spurgeon*

Three Powerful Prayers

what was it that made Asa's reign so remarkable? The answer is found in the fact that from the very start of his reign, he called for the entire nation of Israel to be separate from the surrounding nations. This separation was first manifested in the powerful optics of literally tearing down all of the high places and altars dedicated to idol worship and secondly, the simultaneous national call to seek the God of heaven. Because of this national reform led by the king, the country experienced peace and prosperity. Did Asa use this peace as a time to rest back on his laurels? Certainly not! He used the time to rebuild and strengthen the country. Here is what

Three Powerful Prayers

"When we are experiencing good times, we should take the opportunity to seek God deeper in our lives."

he told the nation: "'Let us build up these towns,' he said to Judah, "and put walls around them, with towers, gates and bars. The land is still ours, because we have sought the Lord our God; we sought Him and He has given us rest on every side.' So they built on every side." (2 Chronicles 14:7 NIV). The lesson taught by Asa's actions is very clear. When we are experiencing good times, we should take the opportunity to seek God deeper in our lives. We must fortify the shallow places of our Christian walk so that the enemy cannot break through! Notice that not only did Asa strengthen the borders around Judah but he made sure that the armies were fully prepared to

"If your day is hemmed in with prayer, it is less likely to come un-raveled."

Cynthia Lewis

Three Powerful Prayers

"We must fortify the shallow places of our Christian walk so that the enemy cannot break through!"

respond to the enemies attacks (v.8)! Oh the lesson for us is so very clear! I imagine that all of the work Asa caused to be done during these peace times were bathed in prayer!

Can you imagine him building borders and training his infantry without first seeking the guidance of God? Of course not!

But the enemy was not oblivious to what was happening inside the nation of Israel! A huge army much greater in strength and numbers than that of Asa's, and led by Zerah the powerful fighter from the country of Cush, had planned an attack on Judah. Asa was now in an untenable situation. He had spent the peace times building up the

> *"We think of prayer as a preparation for work, or a calm after having done work, whereas prayer is the essential work."*
>
> *Oswald Chambers*

country's military bases. But he never expected to be attacked by the massive army of the Cushites composed of undetermined thousands. This powerful army would certainly annihilate their less than a six hundred thousand men of Judah and Benjamin who were armed some with "large shields and spears" and others with "small shields and bows" (v.8). But this is where king Asa revealed the solidity of his force. This is where the years of peace time preparation would finally be put to the test. Asa did not cower in fear of the enemy. All senses indicate that it would have been wise to do so, but fearlessly he went out to meet the enemy. He "took up battle

"He "called to the Lord, his God. . . ." That was the ammunition he used! By ourselves we are not a match for the enemy!"

positions in the Valley of Zephathah near Mareshah" (v.10) against the enemy. Now having postured his army to fight the enemy, look at Asa's next strategic move! He "called to the Lord, his God. . ." That was the ammunition he used! By ourselves we are not a match for the enemy! The historical account did not suggest that Asa gave his men a pepped talk. Once positioned, facing the enemy, Asa did what appeared to some as the unthinkable, he prayed! Looked at his most powerful prayer, *"Lord, there is no one like you to help the powerless against the mighty. Help us, Lord our God, for we rely on you, and in your name we have come against this vast*

263

"All things else being equal, our prayers are only as powerful as our lives. In the long pull we only pray as well as we live."

A.W. Tozer

Three Powerful Prayers

army. *Lord, you are our God; do not let mere mortals prevail against you."* (2 Chronicles 14:10 NIV emphasis added). What a powerful prayer! To examine this prayer in its entirety would require another volume, but let us look very briefly at the antithetical forces at play in his prayer. First his army was miniscule compared to that of the Cushites. Asa knew he was no match for the enemy. But more importantly Asa recognized his powerlessness in contrast to the power of God. He contrasted his weakness with the mighty power of God that was far superior to any earthly force! This is what emboldened Asa to go forward. Hence, the power ignited by Asa's

Three Powerful Prayers

"This is the power that is always unleashed in the wake of the desperate but heartfelt cry out to God."

humble prayer brought about the most stupendous results. *"The Lord struck down the Cushites before Asa and Judah. The Cushites fled, and Asa and his army pursued them. . . Such a great number of Cushites fell that they could not recover; they were crushed before the Lord and his forces. . . ."* (2 Chronicles 14: 12, 13 NIV emphasis added). Asa's prayer resulted in a sweeping victory for Judah but at the same time God was glorified in the victory! This is the power that is always unleashed in the wake of the desperate but heartfelt cry out to God.

Another obscure but nevertheless equally powerful prayer is that uttered by Jonah from the dank and foul depths

"God designed the program of prayer as an 'apprenticeship' for eternal sovereignty with Christ."

Paul E. Billheimer

Three Powerful Prayers

of the stomach of that great fish. Each time I read this biblical story, it never ceases to evoke some visceral reaction in me. I do not like close places. I get very claustrophobic in small spaces. So the thought of what Jonah might have experienced in such close confines is beyond anything I want to imagine. But to give some context to Jonah's prayer, recall that God had commissioned him, a prophet, to preach a message of repentance to the corrupt city of Nineveh. Instead of performing his God-given task, Jonah chose to sail away in the opposite direction towards a city called Joppa (read the story in Jonah chapter 1). On his way to this city, an unusual storm arose. The sailors on board the ship recognized the uniqueness of this encounter. It was a strange convergence of the elements that created the vortex for this sudden change in the tranquility of nature. Jonah, sensing no doubt through his prophetic ability that he was the cause of this literal storm in the lives of these sailors, requested them to throw him overboard. After this action, amazingly, the storm ceased. Whoosh! This reminds me of some of the unnecessary problems we can bring to the lives of others by our own actions! But that's another story! As you know, the moment Jonah hit the water, a "great fish" prepared

Three Powerful Prayers

"God preserves us even when we deserve to be destroyed."

by God caught hold of him and literally swallowed him whole! Now ironically enough, that was divine mercy! God preserves us even when we deserve to be destroyed. Can you imagine Jonah being subjected to the internal esophageal peristaltic waves of this fish after being thrown to the external upheavals of the sea! I think the greatest threat to Jonah's survival was not inside the belly of the fish, but rather being thrown overboard to the open dangers of the storm. Being in the confines of the fish was the beginning of the answer to the prayer he, Jonah, had not yet uttered. This is what God means when he says "Before they call I will answer. . ."

"The driving power, the conquering force in God's cause is God himself. 'Call on me and I will answer thee and show thee great and mighty things which thou knowest not,' is God's challenge to prayer. Prayer puts God in full force into God's work."

E.M. Bounds

Three Powerful Prayers

"Jonah had his moment of clarity from the deep dark recesses of the belly of the fish. From the slushy, raw, stench of his experience, he recognized the power of God."

(Isaiah 65: 24). In the darkness of the innards of the fish, in womblike fashion, Jonah after this incubatory period would experience his rebirth. But this rebirthing would only happen after Jonah had completely understood that God was ultimately in charge. Jonah had his moment of clarity from the deep dark recesses of the belly of the fish. From the slushy, raw, stench of his experience, he recognized the power of God. This is so reminiscent of the prodigal son's moment of epiphany right there in the stench of the pig-pen! Jonah's powerful re-birthing experience only occurred after he called out to God! Yes, that's what prayer is, it's a powerful call out

"Prayer crowns God with the honor and glory due to His name, and God crowns prayer with assurance and comfort. The most praying souls are the most assured souls."

Thomas B. Brooks

Three Powerful Prayers

"The power in Jonah's prayer lies in the fact that he believed God was able to save him even after he was blatantly disobedient."

to God! "... *I cried by reason of mine affliction unto the Lord, and he heard me; out of the belly of hell...."* (Jonah 2: 9 NIV emphasis added). God's response to Jonah's prayer was to create a nauseating upheaval in the belly of the fish, causing it to experience a reversal of the conditions that allowed it to swallow Jonah in the first place, thus heaving him from its gastric confinement. Notice that no stormy conditions surrounded Jonah once he was committed to walking the pathway that God had outlined for him. He finds himself on dry ground with a renewed sense of purpose and a willingness to be obedient to God. The power in Jonah's prayer lies in the

"The devil is not terribly frightened of our human efforts and credentials. But he knows his kingdom will be damaged when we begin to lift up our hearts to God."

Jim Cymbala

Three Powerful Prayers

fact that he believed God was able to save him even after he was blatantly disobedient. In his own words Jonah states "When my soul fainted within me I remembered the Lord; and my prayer came in unto thee, into thine holy temple." (Jonah 2: 7). This is a powerful manifestation of the fact that God still answers our prayers in spite of our guilt.

"God dwells in every abode; He hears every word that is spoken, listens to every prayer that is offered. . . ."

E. G. White

HE ANSWERS!

12

THE FIVE-
DOLLAR PRAYER

". . .road trips were no longer spontaneous family activities but months of measured planning and much praying."

This was in the early nineties. It was the time when changes in the global economy were beginning to affect every household. People were starting to wonder if the cost of fuel heating would ever stop escalating. Gone were the days when one could drive up to the gas station pump and fill up the car for less than ten dollars. These were times when road trips were no longer spontaneous family activities but months of measured planning and

The Five-dollar Prayer

much praying! Of course compared to today's standards, what are you complaining about! It was good back then, gas prices are more than double today! Nevertheless, for a single parent, facing all the economic hardships of the early nineties it was a time of struggle.

In retrospect, I was fortunate in many ways. God had blessed me to complete graduate work at Columbia University. I was now a state and nationally certified medical speech –language pathologist working in a hospital. In previous years my career path was in education. I had taught for many years so it was not surprising that I accepted an evening position

The Five-dollar Prayer

"Every day was bathed in prayer. Any deviation would translate into missing some vital necessity"

two days a week teaching at a local university, in addition to my daytime work at the hospital. This called for masterful juggling of careers. After my daytime work at the hospital I would scurry to pick up my twelve year old daughter from her school and drop her off at the neighborhood library where she dutifully completed her homework. Three hours or so later my teaching assignment over, I would rush back to pick her up from the library. Our day finally ended shortly after nine thirty. And so for several years, this became a way of life for us. But of course, this kind of living required strict adherence to a rigid budget. Every day was bathed in prayer! Any deviation would translate into missing some vital necessity.

One day during one of my dashes between the hospital and the university, I noticed the fuel gauge on the dashboard of my Delta 88 – my prized Oldsmobile – was hovering over the empty mark. My heart sank in my chest. I did not have time to stop at a gas station, and I was running low on cash. Those were the days when you could put three dollars-worth of gas in your car; it wouldn't fill it up, but it would be a substantial enough amount that would cause you to rejoice between twenty minute trips! I pulled over to a gas station taking care not to pull up to the pump just in case I could

The Five-dollar Prayer

"'Lord help me to make it to the school. I'll worry about getting back home afterwards, please keep whatever fuel is in the gas lines flowing so that I can get there. Amen!" This was one of the most desperate prayers I'd ever uttered.'

not fulfil my financial obligation! Engine still running, I was afraid to turn it off! I put the gear in park and I carefully searched my purse. I looked into each crevice, hoping to find some sign of cash or coin. I emptied the contents on the seat of the car, found nothing. Looking at the clock on the dashboard, I knew time was running out. I had to make it to the classroom. I had twenty-five students waiting on me. I breathed a prayer. *"Lord help me to make it to the school. I'll worry about getting back home afterwards, please keep whatever fuel is in the gas lines flowing so that I can get there. Amen!"* This was one of the most desperate prayers I'd ever uttered. I

The Five-dollar Prayer

pulled out of the gas station. Picked up the nearby freeway still praying out loud, *"Lord keep this car running. Take me there safely!"* The car stood the test like any other car on the highway. I made it to the university. I found one of the best parking spots in the parking lot (those were and still are hard to come by in the evenings). I made it to the classroom on time.

Class ended. It was one of my best teaching sessions. I knew it. One student approached me at the end of the class to confirm what I already knew. I was elated. I paused in the corridor to exchange greetings with one of my colleagues. It was an engaging exchange. For a few moments I'd

The Five-dollar Prayer

completely forgotten about my fuel problem. Now as I made my way to the parking lot, approaching my car, a feeling of utter dismay settled over me. What if the car would not start? How will I make it home? Fortunately for me, my daughter was at home and not at the library. She had a school holiday. I had visions of spending the night in the parking lot. Those were not the days of cell phones! I could not call anyone. And even if I could call, it would have been devastatingly embarrassing to tell someone my plight! Despondently I opened the driver's side of the car. I threw my teaching folder on the back seat, placed my head on my hands as

The Five-dollar Prayer

"I am fully persuaded that God not only hears but there are times when He speaks to us directly!"

I gripped the steering wheel. Tears flowing, I cried out to God, *"Please God do something! Help me! I don't know what, but help me!"* I am fully persuaded that God not only hears but there are times when He speaks to us directly! Suddenly, I thought I heard a voice, at first I was not sure it was a voice or my loud thoughts, but it seemed to say *"Open your purse."* I ignored the voice. In my mind I reasoned. There's nothing in the purse. I've already searched every nook and cranny! I started to tap my fingers on the staring wheel, in an effort to distract myself from the strong compulsion to open the purse. But I could not quell that overpowering desire.

285

The Five-dollar Prayer

"But just then the truth hit me with even greater force than the five-dollar bill. God answered my prayer! He provided that five-dollar bill exactly at the time when my faith in His providence needed to be confirmed."

Finally, I grabbed the purse muttering out loud, *"What are you expecting to find?"* I opened the wallet compartment of the purse with an incredulous force of haste. Suddenly a loose piece of paper literally flew out of the purse and hit me on the nose. Inattentively, I reached for the paper and was astonished to see that it was a five-dollar bill! How did this get there? I started to reason in my mind that I must have missed it earlier in my frantic search. But just then the truth hit me with even greater force than the five-dollar bill. God answered my prayer! He provided that five-dollar bill exactly at the time when my faith in His providence needed to be confirmed. I

The Five-dollar Prayer

gingerly started the car. Yes it started as though it had a full tank of gas. I drove to the nearest gas station and bought five-dollars-worth of gas. I thanked God all along the way as I drove. The miracle of that five-dollars-worth of gas extended far beyond that night. I drove the car for one full week before there was any indication from the gas gauge that I needed to refill the tank.

The truth of God's response to our prayers is that even when we prayer with lingering doubt, He still hears and answers.

13

THE GIVING POCKETS

My daughter was in the eleventh grade. Chemistry, Math and Biology were her favorite subjects (things changed later in college). This particular time she had a number of science projects to complete. There were lab supplies that were required by a specific date. Like most teenagers, some distractions occurred and it was not until the day before the deadline for the funds to be turned in, that she informed me of her needs. I did not have the financial where withal. Students were to turn in a check or cash to the science teacher for the already purchased lab supplies. The cost of the supplies were in excess of one hundred dollars. Given our budget, this unplanned exigent would cause irreparable damage to our monthly expenses. I knew the importance of the science project. I knew how this would impact her grades and I did not want to let her down! After all, what parent would do that!

Overwhelmed by the situation, and every other financial hurdle that I anticipated, my emotional world suddenly became unbearable on my back. "Lord can you help me again!"

The Giving Pockets

"I felt that God did an inordinate amount of financial overtime for me, because each time I came to Him it always seemed to be about finances. I wondered if there would ever be a time in my life when I won't have to burden Him with my financial woes."

I felt that God did an inordinate amount of financial overtime for me because each time I came to Him it always seemed to be about finances. I wondered if there would ever be a time in my life when I won't have to burden Him with my financial woes. Let that time come soon Lord!

I think that God must have smiled and shook His head at my simplicity and lack of faith! I can only say now, "Lord help my unbelief?" But going back to the predicament, I did not have a satisfactory solution to the science project problem. As I had so often done in the past whenever I was faced with a difficult situation, if I could not solve it myself, I practiced

The Giving Pockets

the art of distraction. Most times I would bury myself in mundane tasks. I would embark on a spree of cleaning, or rearranging of furniture or painting walls! Somehow, praying was not my first reset button, it always came in as a late third or last resort. This time in question, knowing I could not come up with the needed funds for my daughter's science class, I whispered a half-hearted prayer to God for help, while I buried myself in sorting out a closet that stored a number of my late husband's suits.

It was a little over two years since my husband had passed. I had not quite brought myself to the place where I could dispose of his neatly

The Giving Pockets

tailored suits, and jackets. But this day felt like a good time to immersed myself in that project and not think of my financial deficit. So I opened the closet door and commenced to remove each item of clothing from their hanger. I cannot recall a specific thought that led me to do so, but I stuck my hand in the pocket of a jacket and felt some paper, or so it seemed. I reached for a nearby waste basket in which to transfer any "pocket-garbage" I might encounter. But just as I was about to drop the "garbage" in the waste-basket, my eye caught familiar markings on the paper that elevated it to a higher status than garbage! It turned out to

The Giving Pockets

be two twenty dollar bills that had been slightly crumpled and placed in the pocket of that jacket, precisely when, I'd no idea. But having found that proverbial gold mine, I hastily commenced to search other pockets not even paying heed to the original task of sorting and cleaning. Would you believe! Before I could complete the search of all of the other pockets, I had a net find of almost two hundred dollars! I hastily called my daughter to share the news of this miraculously crazy discovery and at the same time I was crying out, *"Oh God stop! This blessing is too much! You do hear prayers!"* Now what kind of "Thank you prayer" was that? Once my

293

The Giving Pockets

"...The enormity of God's immediate intervention in our situation descended upon us....God continues to intervene in our circumstances even when we are not clear in our thought processes that He will do so."

daughter caught wind of the commotion and what I was shouting to God about, she hurriedly interrupted *"No, don't tell Him to stop, we need more!"* The whole scenario suddenly seemed comical and we both collapsed on the floor among the scattered suits in peals of laughter.

We finally caught our breath and the enormity of God's immediate intervention in our situation descended upon us. My daughter and I fell on our knees right on top of the piled suits and jackets on the floor and thanked God for His miraculous answer!

My daughter was able to pay for her science lab supplies. The

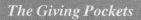

The Giving Pockets

one lesson we learned is that God continues to intervene in our circumstances even when we are not clear in our thought process that He will do so.

14

THE MAN WHO DISAPPEARED

*"I just knew that
I was in the prime
position for a full
"outpouring" that
day and I felt ready
to receive it!"*

I arrived at the parking lot of the church in time to find a parking spot that would ensure freedom from being blocked in at the end of the service. I felt God had started His special blessings on me even before church officially convened. Inside the church, I settled into my favorite seat next to one of the nicest elderly ladies I'd ever met, I just knew that I was in the prime position for a full "outpouring" that day and I felt ready to receive it!

The Man Who Disappeared

The preliminary service began and concluded with a rousing upbeat song. Now it was time for the offering. I reached for my hand bag. I looked to one side of the pew on which I was seated. I could not find it. Maybe it slid to the floor. I searched all around me, but the hand bag was not there. My elderly friend suggested I should check the car. "Of course" I thought, "she's right that's just where it is." I slipped out of my seat and made a hasty trek back to the car. I just knew that my hand bag would be on the front seat. I opened the door, fully expecting to grab my hand bag, but it was nowhere in sight. I looked again frantically this time, under the

297

The Man Who Disappeared

seats of the car, even in small spaces where I knew it could not fit, but just in case it did! Then it hit me! Earlier that morning just before I got in the car, I rested my hand bag on top of the car so that I could adjust the lunch basket on the back seat. It was going to be a pot-luck after service and I'd carefully prepared a casserole for the occasion.

In utter dismay, I slumped in the car fully aware of the impossibility of finding that handbag. That morning I had driven about ten miles to the church through busy streets and crowded alleys oblivious of my lost handbag. I started to take a mental inventory of its contents. Driver's

The Man Who Disappeared

"It's amazing how quickly the enemy can snatch away our peace of mind. In retrospect, I wish I could have calmly recited to myself right at that moment "Great peace have they which love thy law: and nothing shall offend them"
(Psalm 119:165).

license. A credit card. Health insurance card. Sixty-five dollars and possibly some other personal items. I reasoned to myself that I could get by without the sixty-five dollars, but not my personal identifying information! This could fall into the hands of some devious person. Gone was the thrill and joy I felt earlier when I arrived to the church. It's amazing how quickly the enemy can snatch away our peace of mind. In retrospect, I wish I could have calmly recited to myself right at that moment "Great peace have they which love thy law: and nothing shall offend them" (Psalm 119:165). Now totally unnerved by the thought of someone possessing my personal

The Man Who Disappeared

"Feeling utterly defeated I slowly drove away from the church but in my heart I was praying. . ."

item, I hastened back to my seat in the church to share my disastrous plight with my elderly friend. She held my hand and calmly whispered, *"I'll pray that you find it, maybe you should try to retrace your steps back to the house. God knows exactly where your hand bag is at this very moment!"* I thanked her for the advice thinking to myself "fat chance that I'll ever see it again!" But what harm can come in doing as she suggested? Feeling utterly defeated I slowly drove away from the church but in my heart I was praying *"Dear God, please let me find that handbag. It has my personal information that could fall into the wrong hands, please, please God!"*

300

The Man Who Disappeared

I prayed all the way as I drove those ten miles to my home, scouring the streets with hawk's eyes hoping to see some sign of the handbag. Finally I arrived at the house. I looked in every corner of the garage, but the handbag was not there. *"Okay, God, what do I do now?"* Two thoughts occurred to me, call the police station and report the lost handbag just in case some honest person found the handbag, next, call up the credit card company and let them know I'd lost the card. Wow! Great idea! Once inside the house, I reached for the phone to put my thoughts in action. Just then the door-bell rang. I hesitated to answer because, normally at this time I would

The Man Who Disappeared

"Early this morning I was walking along the street and I saw this hand-bag. I picked it up and opened it. I saw a wallet with your driver's license, found your address, and I'm here to return your hand-bag. Everything is in it just as I found it."

be at church, and besides I was not expecting any visitors. So I ignored the bell, but it rang incessantly. This time I hung up the phone and walked slightly annoyed to the front door. I peered through the little window of the door and saw the slightly graying head of a stranger. Opening the door cautiously I inquired who was there. The stranger called my name with a sense of familiarity. He asked if I lived at this residence. I felt emboldened, thinking to myself, "Sure I live here!" I opened the door slightly and with full authority asked the reason for his enquiry. The stranger responded, *"Early this morning I was walking along the street and I*

The Man Who Disappeared

saw this hand-bag. I picked it up and opened it. I saw a wallet with your driver's license, found your address, and I'm here to return your hand-bag. Everything is in it just as I found it."

I stood with my mouth opened. Speechless! I could hardly find enough words to convey my appreciation to the stranger. I offered him the six-five dollars after I'd checked the contents of the hand-bag as he instructed me to do. He refused any recompense for his honesty. He merely expressed his pleasure in returning the lost hand-bag to the rightful owner. As I fiddled to close the bag, I looked up to say another word of "thank you" to the stranger, but he'd left. I hastened

The Man Who Disappeared

down the brick walkway to catch up with him in his car or perhaps walking down the street. I simply wanted to say another "thank you," but he was nowhere to be seen. How did he move so quickly? There was no sign of a bike, motorcycle or car! I recalled that I'd not even heard the sound of a starting car. Who was this man? Where did he go? Why did he disappear so quickly? I did not even catch his name. Did he even tell me his name? I had no answers to these questions. I thanked God for the kindness of the stranger. I thanked God for answering my prayer and that of my elderly friend. I looked at my watch and realized I still had time

The Man Who
Disappeared

*"That was an angel
God sent. He heard
your prayers!"*

to make it back to the church for the preaching service.

I drove back to the church, this time with a joyful heart. As I drove, I scoured the streets again not for the handbag, but in the hopes of catching a glimpse of the stranger. I never saw him. Back in my seat at the church, next to my elderly friend, I recounted to her all of the events that transpired. She squeezed my hand and whispered back, *"That was an angel God sent. He heard your prayers!"*

God is truly creative! He answers prayers in so many different and spectacular ways! I'm learning now to stand back and watch for His ingenious ways of answering prayers.

The Man Who Disappeared

"God is truly creative! He answers prayers in so many different and spectacular ways!"

It's not about doubting anymore, it's about expecting Him to show up for the impossible things. Now I think of the many times God has shown up literally in answer to prayers. I am a firm believer in that God intervenes in our affairs, "The eyes of the Lord are in every place. . ." (Proverbs 15: 3).

YOU DON'T HAVE TO PAY ANY MORE TAXES!

Paying taxes is an obligation that we cannot avoid, even if we feel unjustly burdened! Remember Jesus says *"Give back to Caesar what is Caesar's and to God what is God's"* (Mark 12:17 NIV). But you have to admit there are times when you wish this text was not included in the Bible or that it was not a legal requirement. I felt that way when I was hit by one of the largest tax obligations of my life. It was totally unreal! I just knew it

You Don't Have to Pay Any More Taxes!

was a mistake! Wow! The computers for the Internal Revenue Service must have experienced a glitch! There's no way I could be so indebted to the government!

I picked up the phone and dialed the customer service number of the government agency. Now I'd heard stories of cold IRS personnel whose one quest in life is to capture every penny from tax-paying citizens. I fully expected to be clobbered through the phone – if that were possible. Not surprisingly I heard a crisp clipped voice on the other end. I supplied the appropriate identifying information. Bracing myself, I stated my case. After a period of silence that seemed like an eternity, the official on the other end, walked me through my tax history which, in no way, changed my "owing status." During the whole process of the discussion, I detected a hint of compassion in the tone of the official on the other end. My grip on the phone relaxed a bit. I was able to make a timeline arrangement on how to clear up this debt. I thank the official and hung up the phone.

I was now faced with an obligation that would chip into my budget for a few years to come. *"Lord,"* I cried out, *"This is your case, please help!"* Nevertheless, I commenced making payments on a monthly basis. The added expense dug deeper holes

You Don't Have to Pay Any More Taxes!

into my finances. I could not see a way out of this one. It seemed such an unjust burden. I could think easily of a million reasons why this was not a fair obligation! Why me Lord!

One day in deep desperation I gathered all of the statements from the IRS. I laid them out on the floor of my study. Then I got down on my knees and started praying. It went something like this: *"Father, I have a big problem. Look at these bills. They are more than I can handle. Please help!"* I left the bills laid out on the floor. Every morning and evening, I would go to this place in my study that had now become my hallowed ground, and I would pour out my heart

You Don't Have to Pay Any More Taxes!

"The words of the Psalmist became my reality "Cast your cares on the Lord and He will sustain you. . ." (Psalm 55:22 NIV)."

in earnest before God. This ritual had become a solace for me. I did not receive the answer from God right away, but I kept on praying. Actually, praying over the bills lightened the weight somehow. I thought less about the financial burden as I continued to make those payments. The words of the Psalmist became my reality "Cast your cares on the Lord and He will sustain you. . ." (Psalm 55:22 NIV).

One evening several months later, as I sat down to eat my dinner, the telephone rang. I answered. I heard an unfamiliar but rather upbeat voice requesting to speak with me. The person stated that they were calling from the internal revenue service.

You Don't Have to Pay Any More Taxes!

Oh No! I thought, what else do I owe now? After ascertaining that I was the person sought, the voice continued to say, *"Well, we have rechecked your files and you do not have to continue making those monthly payments."* The words echoed in my ears *"You don't have to continue making those monthly payments!"* One thing I learned from others who had experienced encounters with the IRS, "never argue." Trying to stay as calm as possible I merely requested from the official, *"Could you say that again?"* The official repeated the statement, with the added wish *"Have a good evening ma'am,"* and the phone call ended. I sat down looking

You Don't Have to Pay Any More Taxes!

"You asked God for help! Do not question His miracle!"

at the phone. Then I thought was this a hoax? Was someone playing a trick on me? Shouldn't I have received a letter from the IRS confirming this? Then it flooded back to my mind, *"Your prayers! You asked God for help! Do not question His miracle!"* I walked into the study where the bills laid strewn on the floor. I picked them up raised them towards heaven and shouted *"Thank You! Father! You did it again for me.!"*

I never received a letter from the IRS confirming the phone call neither did I receive another request for payment. All I know is that God settled that debt and I will not question the miracle!

16

THE DAY
DIAL MOVED
BACKWARDS

*"I think of the many
warning signs God
gives us along the
way of life as he
prepares us for some
pending event!"*

I was driving my car one day when an unfamiliar odor seemed to emanate from the engine. It was as if something ominous was going to happen. I was not sure what to make of it so I ignored it and continued driving. In retrospect, I think of the many warning signs God gives us along the way of life as he prepares us for some pending event! When I reached my destination, I heard a strange high pitched sound coming

The Day the Dial Moved Backwards

from the engine and an unfamiliar dashboard icon lit up. I soon realized that all of the warning signals were leading up to an overheating engine. I called the service center at the car dealership and explained the situation. The man on the other end confirmed my suspicions – I had a major car issue. The engine was overheating. He instructed me to turn off the engine, let it cool for about an hour or so and then drive it to the service center. Seemed like an easy enough task so I followed his instructions.

Two hours later I started the car. I was on my way to the service station. Just as the service attendant had assured me, the icon light that

The Day the Dial Moved Backwards

"Everything seemed normal! Whew! I almost wanted to forego the trip to the service center. But something told me this was not God's answer to my problem. He needed to stretch my faith a few more miles!"

warned of the overheating engine was now off. The dial of the thermostat was pointing to the normal section of the gauge. Everything seemed normal! Whew! I almost wanted to forego the trip to the service center. But something told me this was not God's answer to my problem. He needed to stretch my faith a few more miles! I drove for about five of the 30 minute ride, when I noticed the dial was steadily climbing towards the 260^0 mark that signaled "engine overheated." Suddenly all sorts of signals came on the dash board. A message on the dashboard panel told me the power was about to shut down. Immediately the car slowed down to

*The Day the Dial
Moved Backwards*

a snail's pace of less than five miles per hour. I was able to pull over to the side of the road. This time I had a notion that once the engine cooled a bit, I would be able to go again. I was not in an area where I could easily call for a tow truck. Even if I did, it would have been hours before the truck arrived. I had to make it to the service center before closing time. I calculated in my head that my 30 minute drive would turn into an hour and half, and I would still make it before closing if I followed my now formulated plan of "drive-stop-cool-drive". So I waited. The engine cooled. I started again this time I was able to drive for ten minutes before

The Day the Dial Moved Backwards

the bells and whistles told me I had to stop and allow the engine to cool. One thing I had not anticipated was the massive road construction that was causing the traffic to pile up for miles. This actually worked in my favor because the stoppages and the slowly moving traffic bought some reprieve for the engine. I thought of a sign I read somewhere that said "In your messes He blesses!" The mess of traffic pile up was a blessing for me. I couldn't say the same for the other motorists! This reprieve lasted for several minutes. Finally, there was a let up in the traffic, and the road cleared. I should have been happy for this break in the traffic, but

The Day the Dial Moved Backwards

'At that moment I started praying out loud, "Lord you turned the sun back ten degrees for Hezekiah. Please do this for me. Stop that needle from climbing let it go back, please cool the engine!"'

I was dismayed. Since I now had to try to keep up with the flow of traffic I knew that the engine would overheat more quickly. I watched the dial of the thermostat swiftly climb towards the critical number. At that moment I started praying out loud, *"Lord you turned the sun back ten degrees for Hezekiah. Please do this for me. Stop that needle from climbing let it go back, please cool the engine!"* I was afraid to look at the dial after I'd prayed. Would God do this? I sneaked a peek at the dial. It continued to climb. I prayed again, I said *"Lord, I know you can do this, there's no doubt in my mind, but if you don't want to, I'll understand."* This time I took

319

The Day the Dial Moved Backwards

"Just as steadily as the dial had previously moved forward to the critical red number of the temperature gauge, it was now steadily moving backwards towards the normal temperature - the number on the dial that signaled cool."

a bold look at the dial. It continued moving toward that critical number. But I kept on praying, *"Lord You can do this, please turn the temperature dial back towards cool. Thank You."* Then, I saw something! I thought my eyes were playing tricks on me. The dial seemed to have stopped moving forward. My eyes swiftly move from the road to the dial. I watched the dial. I could hardly believe what I was seeing! Just as steadily as the dial had previously moved forward to the critical red number of the temperature gauge, it was now steadily moving backwards towards the normal temperature - the number on the dial that signaled cool. My hands gripped the steering wheel. Tears were streaming down my cheeks. I cried out *"Thank you God! You made the dial to move backwards!"* I did not care if passing motorists thought I had lost my mind as I shouted out my gratitude to God.

I drove the car all the way to the service center with the thermostat dial still registering in the normal setting. Excited with what had occurred, I turned to the mechanic at the service center and asked *"What would make the dial of the thermostat move backwards from hot to cool when the engine is overheating?"* I did not even understand my own question! He looked at me with a perplexed expression, mumbled something.

The Day the Dial Moved Backwards

". . .God resets the button of our lives and allows us a bit more time just to reconnect with Him."

But I quickly, responded, *"Never mind, why should you explain the miracle."* He chuckled. I knew he did not understand. Neither did I. But one thing I knew beyond a shadow of a doubt, God turned the dial back for me. At that moment I realized a truth. Sometimes in His infinite compassion, God resets the button of our lives and allows us a bit more time just to reconnect with Him. We are so often caught up in the busyness of life that our time with God teeters on the brink of zero. If we would slow down and spend more time with Him we would experience a cooling from the cares of this life and some spiritual normalcy. I realized it was not

**The Day the Dial
Moved Backwards**

about the car! It was about me! God was inviting me to slow down and to reconnect with Him.

17

Pull That
Cord Again!

PULL THAT CORD AGAIN!

I was serving as a missionary teacher in the hinterland of South American. It was a missionary out-post to the Davis Indians in a beautiful primitive region called Parima. This region of the country of Guyana, a member of the British Commonwealth, was flanked on either side by the borders of Venezuela and Brazil. Parima was a well-hidden virgin rain forest region at the foot-hills of the majestic Mount Rorima chain. In this relatively culturally

Pull That Cord Again!

"The church house was the epicenter of the village."

uncontaminated Indian reservation region, there were no built up road-ways, no vehicles of any kind except one or two bicycles owned by either missionaries or more fortunate villagers. Only a single well-beaten path marked by the footsteps of the native Indians and missionaries served as the major conduit to the village and the church house. The church house was the epicenter of the village. It not only served as the school-house, but also as the general assembly meeting place where the Village Chief held his council meetings. There was a river that ran through the middle of the village. This river was about a mile and half wide. To me it was an

Pull That Cord Again!

intimidating force even though it seemed gentle enough to those who were accustomed to navigating its waters in little dugout canoes. I was petrified of the brown water. Who knows what frightful creatures lurked under the surface. Nevertheless this water was vital to the existence of humans, animals and crops.

It was not unusual to see the villagers do their laundry, take their showers and enjoy recreational swims right there at the edge of the river. It was home. But for me the river remained a formidable force. I was not a swimmer and I had no knowledge of navigating a canoe across the river. The nearest village from our location

Pull That Cord Again!

". . .it was the greatest privilege to work with fellow missionaries who undoubtedly were spirit-filled and possessed a passion for service."

was about three hours away by canoe that is, if the canoe were out fitted with an outboard engine. But travel time rose exponentially if undertaken by row boat. As one would imagine, visits to the nearby village were not frequent occurrences.

So it was at the age of nineteen, I had undertaken one of the most exciting and scary experiences of my life – living and working in a region devoid of every modern convenience I'd ever known. No cars, no taxis, no buses, no telephones no easily accessible bathroom conveniences! But in spite of these "denials," it was the greatest privilege to work with fellow missionaries who undoubtedly were

Pull That Cord Again!

"In this primitive environment, I learned many valuable skills of survival without modern conveniences that I could never have acquired elsewhere."

spirit-filled and possessed a passion for service. I was especially awed by the zeal and tender compassion of the pastor and his wife who adopted every missionary teacher as part of their own family.

The students were eager to learn about the love of God as well as every new math and science concept. Frequently, I had to utilize a student as an interpreter during some class instructions. In this primitive environment, I learned many valuable skills of survival without modern conveniences that I could never have acquired elsewhere. But my greatest lesson yet was to be learned on the river, in a canoe.

Pull That Cord Again!

It so happened that I came down with a strange illness. Fever, chills and anxiety. We had no skilled medical help available in our village. The closest health-care out post manned by a nurse was in the nearest village about three or four hours distance down the river by motor boat (canoe). Since no one knew the nature of my illness, the best plan was to get me to the village as soon as possible. The pastor's wife who had some skills in nursing although not fully trained, made the necessary arrangements and was going to be my travel companion. The trip entailed a short thirty or forty minute stint by rowboat to the opposite side of the river to a landing where we

Pull That Cord Again!

"I silently repeated the familiar lines from the twenty-third psalm, "The Lord is my shepherd I shall not want."

would transfer to the motor powered canoe. Early that morning, we made the first leg of the trip uneventfully. Our navigator and guide assisted in transferring our light load to the engine powered boat. As instructed by our skilled navigator, I took up my position seated in the middle of the boat the pastor's wife in the rear while the navigator, our "captain" as we called him was at the helm. We calculated that since we had an early start we would reach the village long before we encountered the scorching rays of the midday sun. We prayed. I silently repeated the familiar lines from the twenty-third psalm, "The Lord is my shepherd I shall not want."

Pull That Cord Again!

The "captain" pulled the cord to start the engine. It sputtered. He pulled it again it caught and the chugging started. The water around the engine churned and we were on our way! Wrapped in the blankets provided by my travel companion, I nestled down as comfortably as I could praying for the time to pass quickly. The occasional reassuring songs and conversational exchanges from the pastor's wife helped to pass the time.

We were about twenty minutes into the journey when almost without warning, there was a change in the rhythm of the engine and then silence. The captain fiddled with the motor. I was not too concerned because I

Pull That Cord Again!

"Drift and row. Drift and row. So the journey continued....We were nowhere near to our destination."

trusted his skills. However, after he pulled the cord to start the engine a few times, and the engine did not respond, I realized that our situation was getting grave. With a few exchanges in his halting English, it was clear that since the motor was not starting, we would have to drift down the river and row. Our "captain' would have to do the rowing. This was going to be a tough task for one person. Drift and row. Drift and row. So the journey continued. Two hours, three hours passed. We were nowhere near to our destination. The stress of the new turn in the events, weighed heavily on me and I felt weaker and a growing sense of panic. Although surrounded by

Pull That Cord Again!

much water we had a limited supply of fresh drinking water and food. The heat of the midday sun started to beat down on us in the canoe. To shift posture would be a sure way of capsizing the canoe. We had to maintain our positions. My thoughts drifted to my homeland thousands of miles away. I thought of my parents. I longed for them. What if I were to die on this river? I did not stand a chance of survival. There were no life jackets and I could not swim. No one will find us. I started praying as I never had before. *"Lord, please save us. Lord help the engine to start. Whatever you do don't let us die out here in this brown river, please God!"* Fear gripped my heart.

*Pull That
Cord Again!*

*"We each sought
the one Linguis-
tic Equalizer! We
prayed the same
prayer from our
vantage points, even
though we did not
know the similarity
of our prayers at the
time."*

I was petrified of the brown-colored river. It seemed more threatening than before. *"Please God, save us!"* I kept on praying in my heart. Everyone in the canoe was quiet. I could not muster up any conversation as I was too weak from my illness. Besides, we were all linguistically challenged. Our "captain's" English was limited and neither the pastor's wife nor I had any functional command of his native Arecuna language. We were in a predicament! But we each sought the one Linguistic Equalizer! We prayed the same prayer from our vantage points, even though we did not know the similarity of our prayers at the time.

Pull That Cord Again!

We continued to drift down the river. The waters were somewhat calm. That was a blessing. But soon it would become dark. In that part of the country, sunset came suddenly because the sun dropped behind the mountain almost without warning. A crazy thought came to my mind. I wondered if the "captain" would pull the cord to the engine one more time. We had drifted and rowed for well over eight hours. Later I learned from my travel companion that she too was praying that our "captain" would "pull the cord" to start the engine again. We had been drifting in silence for many hours. No verbal exchanges passed between us, except for those

Pull That Cord Again!

"I continued with my obsessive prayer. "Lord save us!""

times when my travel companion checked to see how I was doing. I have to admit that her presence gave me great assurance as I knew she was a woman of prayer.

It was growing darker. The river was a threatening expanse of blackness. I was filled with unspeakable apprehension! *"God, please, please save us!"* Will we survive this ordeal! I continued with my obsessive prayer. *"Lord save us! Tell the captain to 'pull the cord' again."* I didn't know at the time why I had the obsession with the cord. We all knew that something was wrong with the engine. So what good would it do to pull the cord again? But the same words of the pray continue to swirl around in my head *"Lord, please let him 'pull the cord' again."* Then without warning and in total silence the "captain" reached out, grabbed the cord attached to the engine and pulled! Lo and behold, the familiar sputter from the engine was heard. The spark caught. The engine continued running. The propeller started churning the water. The canoe made a lurch forward and glory be to God we were moving! The engine continued churning as if it had received new life! Two hours later in the dead of the night we arrived at our destination. No sooner had the "captain" guided the canoe to the landing, without any warning the

**Pull That
Cord Again!**

engine stopped running. There was silence, but we cheered. We thanked God! He had brought us safely to the village where I would receive the medical help I needed.

Later that night I learned that one of the mechanics in the village who had examined the engine was dumbstruck that the engine ever started. He asked our "captain," *"How did this engine run? There is no way it could have worked without the plug!"* The captain knew that the vital part had fallen off into the river shortly after we had started out. He did not want to alarm us. He too had been praying. My travel companion was praying. I was praying. After many hours of

"God is especially attentive to the combined prayers of His people."

drifting on the river, "captain" felt an overpowering urge to "pull the cord again." We believed that it was at the precise moment of the convergence of our prayers that God directed our "captain" to pull the cord again! There is no doubt in my mind that God is especially attentive to the combined prayers of His people. No wonder Jesus declares in Matthew 18: 19 *". . . .That if two of you shall agree on earth as touching anything that they shall ask, it shall be done for them of my Father which is in heaven."*

CPSIA information can be obtained
at www.ICGtesting.com
Printed in the USA
BVHW091940131118
533029BV00016B/138/P